# I DON'T
# BELIEVE IT!

I DON'T
BELIEVE IT!

# I DON'T BELIEVE IT!

## Original Complaints
### of
## TUNBRIDGE WELLS

Edited by
Nigel Cawthorne

GIBSON SQUARE

This edition published for the first time by Gibson Square in 2020

UK  Tel:    +44 (0)20 7096 1100
    Fax:    +44 (0)20 7993 2214

US  Tel:    +1 646 216 9813
    Fax:    +1 646 216 9488

Eire Tel:   +353 (0)1 657 1057

info@gibsonsquare.com
www.gibsonsquare.com

ISBN   978-1783340644

Printed by CPI.

# CONTENTS

# INTRODUCTION

Last year, I was delighted to make more friends than I lost with the publication of *Outraged of Tunbridge Wells*, where I compiled for the first time choice letters of complaints from the era of Agatha Christie and P.G. Wodehouse from the *Tunbridge Wells Advertiser*. It seemed that the only people up in arms about it were, in fact, well… from Tunbridge Wells. A Mrs P. Benson protested vehemently on Amazon that I had put 'another nail in the coffin of good old fashioned British decency and fair play.' Curious to discover in what way I might have pleased P. Benson more, I had a peak at her other reviews. I was not a little crestfallen to discover that a top favourite (five stars) of the outraged Tunbridgewellian was a Koolpak to soothe 'those swollen knuckles after giving hubby a good thrashing for leaving the toilet seat raised.' My book, relegated to the company of Zimmer frames ('A potential death trap', one star as well) had even failed the club-my-husband-over-the-head test. On the other hand, perhaps I myself had come off lightly.

I was, therefore, a little surprised when my publisher asked me to compile yet another collection of letters on the very British art of complaining. I suspect this might well have had something to do with the appreciative book reviews and radio interviews that *Outraged of Tunbridge Wells*

attracted, and their thinking that these outweighed the offense the book had caused.

Having a carefully-crafted moan has had a long and distinguished history in Britain—arguably one of almost a millennium. It is well understood that taxes and death are the two certainties of life. While death is largely not much fun, we Brits understood from early on that taxation has a small edge on death in that it comes hand-in-hand with an inalienable right to splutter, rail, and rant about anything and everything when that hard-earned cash is being misappropriated. The fact that it should come with such a right, at any rate, has been one of the main drivers of British history. The principle found an early expression in Magna Carta from where it has grown spectacularly successfully to become the democratic side of the tax coin in Britain.

The expression 'disgusted of Tunbridge Wells' is therefore as quintessentially British as Magna Carta. Nowhere is the connection between taxpaying and complaining more intimate than at home. The Tunbridgewellians paid taxes like everyone in Britain, and rather a lot in their estimation, and sat at home with little else to do but consider the daily filth they were subjected to. They had the time to let their rage come to the boil very effectively.

In this book I seek out the letter writers who, while they did not themselves live in Tunbridge Wells necessarily, were definitely 'of Tunbridge Wells' when they wrote to their local newspaper. There are a few familiar names that fans of *Outraged* may recognise. The fanatic M. E. Welldon—for

whom sin, smut and Armageddon loomed
everywhere in peaceful Tunbridge Wells—turns out
to have written letters to other papers, too, and
remained as keen to warn their readers about the
wrath of god. A new star is Colonel C. Pulley who
precipitated a lively debate on hem lines for young
girls and gave the 'Fascisti' his somewhat reluctant
thumbs up before his death in 1925.

What all these writers have in common is an
urgent desire to make crystal clear what they think is
wrong rather than just give vent to the vehemence
of their emotions. Before the internet turned
complaining into a channel of snarkiness, trolling
and vicious shouting, Britain had the subtle skill of
invective down to an art after centuries of getting on
top of their pesky royals. Despite the sometimes
serious subject matter, things are usually treated in a
light-hearted manner – indeed, with a proper British
insouciance. That is, a mixture of a stiff upper lip
and a lower one quivering with a suppressed
chuckle.

'Permit me, through your valuable Journal'
begins one letter, as many do, worrying that they are
trespassing too much on the paper's space. Yet these
self-effacing openings soon give way to prolific
amounts of roaring with grievous complaints.
Contrary to the humble words, trespassing on as
much of the paper as possible was exactly what was
on the minds of the letter writers. It is their neigh
sacred rescue duty to 'endeavour to rouse our local
governors from the state of helpless lethargy into
which they seem to have fallen,' or by extension

other public events or nuisance created by their neighbours and not checked by the authorities.

Short sentences slam down with precision. For example, one writer responding to a letter by a working mother who argues against the foundation of a charitable retreat for cats — as World War I is raging in the background — declares that what she 'didn't know on the subject [of cats] wasn't worth knowing.' She sweetly continues her letter to agree that there is merit in a crèche for working mothers. Instantly, however, in the next line the letter turns personal, as she explains that her agreement is induced by 'the spectacle of numbers of young children ... left outside public houses while their working mothers are drinking.' Without outright condemnation, the author has remained well-mannered, while taking no hostages as she has made cats seem perhaps rather deserving after all.

The letters written during the two World Wars are of particular interest. While the world is in flames about them, the sturdy letter writers continue to air their paltry grumbles. They come thick and fast the beginning of World War I until paper shortages and censorship limit their scope. Paper rations and other restrictions also curtail the complaints in World War II, though some gems still get through.

During World War I, one Tonbridge woman wrote in on the serious problem of Tunbridge Wells' men being 'few in proportion to the population have come forward at this moment of life and death' while another railed against 'the superfluity of trees in the roads, shutting out air, light and sunshine', and a third queries why there is no Channel Tunnel as this would surely have clinched the war already. During World War II, closing cinemas on the Sabbath would save the Empire, while rancour is expressed about 'weeds growing without restriction in neighbouring gardens and allotments.' These peeves did not let up despite being in the first line of attack from the Germans as all these letter writers wrote in to the *Kent & Sussex Chronicle* (covering the Tunbridge Wells area), the *Dover Express*, the *Folkestone, Hythe, Sandgate and Cheriton Herald*, the *Kentish Chronicle*, the *Kentish Gazette*, the *Maidstone Telegraph*, the *West Kent Guardian*, the *Whitstable and Herne Bay Herald* and the *Kent Messenger*, the Kent newspapers from which the letters in this volume are taken.

These letters are also postcards from the past, giving us a fascinating glimpse into the lives of ordinary people, most whom are now long dead. This is the fabric of real life, not the tailored cloth you get in the history books. It is not only the heart-felt sarcasm and pomposity but also this that makes them enjoyable, and enjoyable to read again and again. Through them we obliquely see the Great Depression, the growth of labour movement, the onset of the Suffragettes, the emergence of Fascism and the hardship of the World Wars.

Ultimately, we recognise ourselves in these writers. Even in the twenty-first century, Britain is still a large country dotted with many small towns. Long may there be outrage!

SHEER

INEPTITUDE

## UNSEATED

SIR — I do not agree that in most things the wishes of more recent residents are well considered in Tunbridge Wells. Several letters of mine have appeared requesting seats upon one or both sides of Mount Pleasant road. Three summers have come and gone since, but seats are conspicuous by their absence.

**J. G. POVEY**
*Kent & Sussex Courier*
September 21, 1923

\*\*\*

## KEY INCOMPETENCE

SIR — It is somewhat surprising that the fire-engines are so very badly managed. This morning, it was about half-an-hour before the key to the engine-house could be found. Together with time lost in providing horses (as was the case to-day), they generally arrive too late to be of any service, the premises being destroyed before they arrived.

**A CONSTANT READER**
*Gravesend and Milton Express*
April 25, 1835

## TAD SOP

SIR — There is no truth in the assertion [above],

that half an hour elapsed before the keys of the engine-house could be found. They were never lost; and it may be some satisfaction to your correspondent to be informed that it is next to impossible that any delay should ever occur, there being no less than nine keys of the engine-house, one in possession of the foreman of the engine, and each fireman—the other two in my possession.

The first intimation I had of the fire was from Mr Mace, who immediately, at my request, took the trouble of riding to the house of the foreman of the engine. It wanted five minutes to one when Mr Mace gave me the alarm, and the engine was started at ten minutes past one. Unfortunately, the post-horses were all out, and we were sent two pair of odd horses with two stable hands. One of the horses fell, soon after leaving town, and the fire engine proceeded with three only. After passing Southfleet Church, through the awkwardness of the man who rode the fore-horse (though warned of the danger by the foreman) the carriage of the engine came in contact with a post and the pole was broken. As soon as the horses could be disengaged from the carriage, it was driven to the fire, by the firemen. It was our misfortune, and not our fault.

**R. TADMAN**

*Gravesend and Milton Express*
May 2, 1835

\*\*\*

## MUCK CENTRAL

SIR — 'He that doeth nothing, doeth ill': so I
will endeavour to rouse our local governors from
the state of helpless lethargy into which they
seem to have fallen. Surely our parochial officers
must be little blessed with any acute perceptions
in the senses of sight and smell, or they could
not suffer the disgracefully filthy state in which
some of the streets of Greenwich have recently
been, longer to continue. A short time since
public attention was directed through your
columns to the grievances caused by pigs
wandering at large. The same evil however, still
continues. In addition, mud has been raked into
heaps and left (to dry I suppose) for a week or
more before taken away. We have the washings
of Blackheath, the filth so nicely swept and
cleaned from our aristocratic neighbours in
Stockwell-street, the drainings of London-street,
all concentrated in Church-street.

**GNAT**
*West Kent Guardian*
October 21, 1843

## STENCH LOOKERS

SIR — Permit me, through your valuable Journal,
to direct attention to a circumstance which I
think highly important to the Inhabitants of

Woolwich: I mean the unpleasant smell arising from certain drains in the immediate vicinity of King-street, William-street and others. That in King-street is really beyond endurance. When I and a few other parishioners complained of it we were told it should 'be looked to;' it was accordingly 'looked to,' or rather 'looked at,' but nothing else was done.

**OBSERVER**
*West Kent Guardian*
April 21, 1844

## ETON FOOLS

SIR — I was surprised to see in your Journal a letter signed 'Disciplinarian,' respecting the head master at the King's School. Yes, that gentleman was perfectly right by persons who are not opposed to corporal punishment. But it was not flogging that was at first objected to, but the punishment of an innocent lad.

Disciplinarian contradicts himself in a great portion of his letter. What on earth does it matter to the inhabitants of Canterbury what is done at the great school at Eton? If that argument was correct, just because they were a school of simpletons (I don't say they are), Disciplinarian would have the scholars of the King's School the same.

[The subject of corporal punishment having been we think sufficiently discussed, we must

17

beg to decline inserting any further
communications.—Ed.]
**JAMES AYERS**
*Kentish Chronicle*
October 22, 1859


## TOWN-HALL COUP

SIR — On entering the Guildhall today, and
making my way to the accustomed standing-place
of the burgesses, I was told by town sergeant
Davey that I must not go in. I then attempted to
open the opposite door when the hall-keeper, Mr
Biggs, said, 'You cannot go in, Sir.'
I said I would go in, it was a common hall and as
I was a burgess no order could prevent me from
entering while there was room. I dared the
officials and walked in, Mr Biggs and Inspector
Spratt following. The inspector put his hand on
me and said, 'Mr Carter, you cannot remain.' I
replied, 'I protest against your removing me;
mind, if you do it, it shall be by force.' I then
enquired of the hall-keeper by whose authority I
and my fellow citizens were refused to occupy
that part of the hall, which from time
immemorial they had had an undoubted right to?
He said, 'By order of the Mayor, Mr Carter.' I
then replied, 'Remain I will, and I protest in the
name of my fellow citizens, against any such
order,' daring the officials to remove me. I was
then allowed to remain.

**S. CARTER**
*Kentish Chronicle*
November 16, 1861

## PITCH-BLACK TOSSERS

SIR — Will you permit me to draw attention to a long-standing and most intolerable nuisance. I allude to the assembling on the Sabbath of a number of the lowest blackguards in the town on the towing path of the River Medway, near the barrack pier, playing 'pitch and toss,' and insulting every respectable female that passes.
**J.S.**
*Maidstone Telegraph*
November 21, 1863

## STREETLIGHTGATE

SIR — Having made an application to the Town Council for permission to build an ornamental entrance from the path on Dane John to be lighted at night by two lamps, I hear today my request has been refused, in consequence of which, as I cannot carry out the plan I intended, I am compelled to abandon the project. The members of the Council would have been wiser, in my opinion, to have permitted the improvement, as by their refusal the public lose the benefit of the extra rates and taxes, and the protection of two additional lamps.

**CHARLES GOULDEN**
*Kentish Chronicle*
January 7, 1865

## CRIME MAGNETS

SIR — A paragraph appeared in last week's Journal, stating that the inhabitants of Herne Bay were dissatisfied that no magistrate had yet been selected for the town. We beg to inform you, in order that the public shall not thereby be misled, that we find the opinion of the town to be, and without exception, that no magistrate is necessary or required. It has never been so entirely free from vagrancy, drunkenness, or any other misdemeanour. Strange as it may be and appear, it has even been less so, since we ceased to have any magistrate.

**THOMAS BAILEY, ALEX. WETHERELL**
*Whitstable Times and Herne Bay Herald*
July 12, 1873

## GAS WORK FILTH

SIR — I am constrained to call your attention to a most abominable nuisance in this place. Those residing or staying here are constantly annoyed by a very filthy and unhealthy smell proceeding, and I should fancy, arising from the Gas Works. I have heard people complain the drainage was bad, when generally the sole cause of complaint has been what I state. The Town Commissioners should at once see into the matter.

**PRO BONO PUBLICO**

*Whitstable Times and Herne Bay Herald*
October 3, 1874

## BELL BAIT

SIR — Can any of your readers inform me what steps should be taken to prevent the intolerable nuisance which is caused by boys and girls ringing the street door bells of tradesmen on Sundays? My own bell was rung unnecessarily no less than sixteen times last Sunday. Where are the police that the behaviour of these young people is not better looked after?

**DISTURBED**

*Whitstable Times and Herne Bay Herald*
January 5, 1889

## RUINATION ENGINES

SIR — Cannot something be done to prevent some, at least, of the traction engines going up the Parade? This morning we had four before 8 am and yesterday we had them all day long. Then we had the steam roller in the other street close by. In the midst of the Season it is too bad, and of course prevents those staying who have come to 'old time' Dover. Last and previous week we had steam rollers every day. Surely this work could be done in the autumn or winter. It is hurtful to lodging house keepers and ruination to Dover.

**ONLY ONE**
*Dover Express and East Kent News*
August 7, 1903

## SHELTER SHOCK

SIR — Being a constant visitor to Dover and a lover of the Sea Front, I am rather astonished you have not more shelters. I can only count four. Seats are plentiful; but the shelter is more convenient on a showery morning.

**A LOVER OF DOVER**
September 15, 1902
*Dover Express and East Kent News*
Friday, 19 September 1902

## DEATH-TRAP CHURCHES

SIR — Ventilation wants attending to in your churches. A stifling atmosphere, inducing headache and sleepiness, is most deleterious to the health of all taking part.

**A VISITOR**
*Kent & Sussex Courier*
November 24, 1905

## NUTSHELL

SIR — What does Dover want from a resident's point of view? On the Sea Front it wants quiet and cleanliness. The shelters should be cleaner and be kept clean by taking away the dirty gratings and putting cement. The children and newspaper boys should not be allowed to yell, and people in the covered seats should not be annoyed by children playing by running in and out of them. If children want to exercise themselves let them go on to the beach. Rotten old boats that are no use should be taken away.
**RESIDENT**
*Dover Express and East Kent News*
May 19, 1911

## STAFF RESIGNATION

SIR — The time is now approaching when dwellers in Folkstone are called upon to put up with an annual pest in the shape and sound of children who come, sometimes twice or three times every evening, and scream carols out of tune and with raucous voices on the doorsteps. These children usually ring the bell several times to make servants answer the door to them. The nuisance usually begins about December 1, and goes on till Christmas Day. I have nothing to

23

say against legitimate carol singers and trained choirs; in fact, I am pleased to hear them, but surely something might be done to prevent the nuisance I have mentioned?

**RESIDENT**
*Folkestone, Hythe, Sandgate, and Cheriton Herald*
December 6, 1913

## PAINT SHOCK

SIR — About four or five months ago, half the pillar and wall letter boxes were painted and certainly not before they wanted it. Then presumably the stock of red paint gave out?

**QUID NUNC**
*Kent & Sussex Courier*
September 16, 1921

## LAZY SODS

SIR — What is wrong with the manhood of the nation that so many of our charming rivers are allowed to waste their health-giving attributes. Can't you boom your river or do the boys funk a lock or two, preferring to laze on the boat cushions talking sweet nothings to a pretty girl. The waste of waterways in this country is a scandal.

**HOMO**
*Kent & Sussex Courier*
October 25, 1921

## PATH ATTACK

SIR — Officials have left the paths on the Common in such an uncomfortable condition. The loose shingle is most painful to the feet. Why cannot these uncomfortable paths be asphalted? Surely also an appointed scavenger should clear away the disgraceful amount of papers left round the seats under trees and elsewhere where people have enjoyed their picnic, but left all their empty bags and waste. I should like to know also why the gates of Holy Trinity churchyard are often locked by 6 o'clock, or why they are locked at all?

**A. M. T**

*Kent & Sussex Courier*

August 31, 1923

## CHATTERING CASES

SIR — I took the opportunity to be at the opening of the Band season, knowing there would be some first-class music. I was disgusted at some ladies during the programme. They did nothing else but talk. The louder the band played the louder they talked. Worse some Councillors did the same.

**DISGUSTED**

*Kent & Sussex Courier*

June 29, 1923

25

## ROUNDABOUT HORROR

SIR — It is time that Tunbridge Wells formed a protest to the Lord of the Manor against the very trying music that goes on all day to cheer on the roundabouts. Last Bank Holiday I tried in vain to escape this aimless horrible sound, but its penetrating voice followed me even to the cemetery.

**LOVER OF MUSIC**

*Kent & Sussex Courier*
August 24, 1923

## SCREECHING WINDS

SIR — The neighbourhood which suffers from the organ stretches far and wide, for its penetrating, grinding and screeching is carried by the West wind well beyond district.

**DISGUSTED**

*Kent & Sussex Courier*
September 7, 1923

## SALVATION HELL

SIR — All your correspondents overlook the main point. Tunbridge Wells is a health resort for nerve cases and rest cures, who stay in hotels

facing just that part of the common which the
Salvation Army Band chooses for its noisy,
nerve-racking performances. In what other resort
of invalids would this be permitted?

**A CATERER FOR VISITORS**
*Kent & Sussex Courier*
June 6, 1924

## TOOTH ACHE

SIR — Having applied for the post of dental
mechanic at the Dover Dental Clinic, I have since
been informed that the post was filled by the
mechanic from the Folkstone Clinic. Do you
think it is right that a man out of work for two
years and with twelve years' experience, should
be jumped over? One thing—a Dover man out
of work has not a chance.

**G. H. JENKINS**
*Dover Express and East Kent News*
April 11, 1924

## GLOBAL PITS

SIR — I have been to burial places in several
parts of our vast Empire: Africa, India, British
Guiana, West Indies, Ceylon, Egypt, etc, and can
say in all sincerity that in none of them, whether
English, Mohammedan, or Little Dutch dorps in
the Transvaal, have I seen anything approaching

27

the neglect and desolation of the spot called 'Gods Acre' in Royal Tunbridge Wells.

**E. A. C. HORNER**
*Kent & Sussex Courier*
May 23, 1924

## EGO-MANIACS

SIR — £10,000 for a house for the Band to please Councillor Berwick. Not a penny for houses for the working man to please Councillor Worsdale. What the ratepayer think you could not print.

**AN OLD RATEPAYER**
*Kent & Sussex Courier*
May 15, 1925

## BREAD SCAM

SIR — Why should the quarter loaf be only reduced from 10½d to 10d in Tunbridge Wells when in London bread is 9d and 8½d, and in Tunbridge Wells Co-operative Society is selling at 9½d? Nothing dreadful has happened to the baking industry in London yet, and there is no reason to believe that all the disasters predicted will happen in Tunbridge Wells. If the Co-operative Society's loaf is considered to be unhygienically produced, I have no doubt the Co-operators will be willing to join in any investigation with the quality of the article or the cost of production, including wages.

**CONSUMER**

*Kent & Sussex Courier*
October 16, 1925

## MILK BILK

SIR — Already dairymen are charging winter prices for milk, but when the corresponding summer prices are due, the reduction is made two or three weeks after London. Consumers are, therefore, compelled to pay an additional month at higher prices. It is time that an 'Association of Housekeepers' was formed to combat this.

**A VICTIMISED HOUSEKEEPER**

*Dover Express and East Kent News*
August 2, 1929

## BEASTLY ARMS

SIR — As a bit of economy, if the authorities were to scrap the beastly arms of the shelters, it would give room for 32 more visitors to sit in comfort in the four shelters. I often see folks bring old newspapers to keep the cold wind off even in summer time.

**ANOTHER YORKSHIRE TYKE**

*Dover Express and East Kent News*
February 4, 1927

## DEADLY BUS RACES

SIR — The election will soon be upon us, and the rate payers of this town will before long be inundated with promises that are never carried out once the candidate is elected. We are having a bridge widened for motorists and motor buses to race up and down our High Street, and nothing whatever is being done to widen at St Stephen's, where six buses and sometimes more are each side of the street, making it difficult for motorcars or pedestrians to get through. Who is responsible for this? Surely our Councillors have some control over the town? There will be a day of reckoning sooner or later, when one sees those buses looping the loop at the station, others doing the merry-go-round at the War Memorial. Isn't it possible to have a depot at one end, say Ashdown Forest, and the other end Shipbourne Common, with a ten-minute service through the town with stopping places at the Star and Garter, Rose and Crown, Angel Hotel and the Railway station? This would do away with the racecourse composed of buses lined up to race each other at a given signal. Then comes the cutting in and the road is impassable. Councillors, ex-Councillors and gentlemen who are likely to put up at the next election, remember every life saved is a vote for you.

**J. H. BURT**
*Kent & Sussex Courier*
February 18, 1927

## BUS AGONY

SIR — As a comparative newcomer to Tunbridge Wells I should like to draw the attention of your readers to the fact that I have seen no signals in this town to show were buses stop. I have often watched people in the High Street quite at a loss.

**DISGUSTED**

*Kent & Sussex Courier*
June 2, 1933


## MINE FIELD

SIR — The numerous references to miners in the columns of the local press would make it appear that Kent is a modern 'Eldorado' to which miners of other parts of the country flock. Those in charge of future developments would be well advised not to lose sight of the fact that Kent is not the only coalfield in the country and that when work gets more plentiful in other parts it will not be so easy to exploit the labour market as seems to be the case at the present time.

**H. KEENAN**

*Dover Express and East Kent News*
January 3, 1930

## PLANET OF THE DOGS

SIR — Is Tunbridge Wells dead? Yes it died years ago. All gone to the dogs. Dogs in the highways, dogs in the recreation grounds, dogs yapping around all day and sometimes all nights. Dogs' filth everywhere.

**DISGUSTED**

*Kent & Sussex Courier*
September 8, 1933

## MORTARLY BORED

SIR — To the Wells Repertory Players: 'The Knight of the Burning Pestle' is certainly not the type of classic to appeal to the average man in the street. In the first production of the opening season you so far experiment as to give us a show which 95 per cent of us were unable to understand. True, our tastes may be plebeian, but we do represent the bulk of your audience. Please do not take this as being the opinion of one person, because I can assure you that I would not bother if such were the case.

**R. PURNELL**

*Kent & Sussex Courier*
March 23, 1934

## DISCONCERTING TRIPE

SIR — What appeared to me, and probably
countless other Dovorians, on Jubilee Day
was its utterly inglorious ending by what had
been officially notified as a 'Display of
Fireworks.' Well, one came away feeling
ashamed of one's town. A more disgusting
and disappointing 'display' of a succession of
sputtering 'so-called' fireworks could hardly
be imagined. To place such an exhibition of
'tripe' before the townspeople is still yet
another example of 'Anything will do for
Dover!' Better shows can be seen on Guy
Fawkes' night given by boys of the town.
Who was responsible for it all? The
intermittent flashes may have been a trifle
disconcerting to the passing shipping. And we
lay claim to being the premier Cinque Port
[cradle of the royal navy]!
**DOVORIAN**
*Dover Express and East Kent News*
May10, 1935


## EGGSTRAORDINARY

SIR — With reference to the complaint
brought before last week's Council meeting
about a dustbin having been mistreated, I also
wish to complain. A hen of mine has laid an
egg, thicker at one end than the other. It was a
brand spanking new un. Should not the creature

be more careful? Or is this a matter for its approved society?

**PRO BONO PUBLICO**
*Dover Express and East Kent News*
May 15, 1936

## TYRANT WISH

SIR — During the last few years I have lived in various towns in the South of England but never have I lived in various town in the South of England but never have I known streets to be so filthy in this respect as in Tunbridge Wells. Should we ever have a Dictator in this country it is to be hoped that one of his first measures would be to ban the keeping of dogs in towns.

**CLEANLINESS**
*Kent & Sussex Courier*
April 28, 1939

## BUMS WITHOUT SEATS

SIR — Many thanks for your remarks upon the wanton damage done to the seats placed on the East Cliff by Mr Hill. I trust that other and more wanton acts of vandalism may be brought to light and punished. I noticed the other day that one of six seats, placed on the further extremity of the Cliff by the kindness of Mr

Solomon, was pulled up completely and thrown down the hill.

**UNSEATED**

*Whitstable Times and Herne Bay Herald*
June 8, 1872

## UNPLEASANT SAND

SIR — I was amongst the many visitors to Tankerton on Monday last. I was delighted with the place, and found only one thing wanting, and that is a few more bathing-machines that *can* be run into the sea when the tide is ebbing, so that bathers have not to run a distance from thirty and fifty yards before reaching the water. Being one of the unfortunate individuals who were subjected to this unpleasantness, I venture to suggest that something be done to remedy it in future.

**T. L. C.**

*Whitstable Times and Herne Bay Herald*
August 9, 1884

## DREDGING FOR COMPLIMENTS

SIR — Mr Churchill [First Lord of the Admiralty] paid a visit to Dover Harbour yesterday, but it was noticed by many that the noisy dredger was kept quiet until he left. Will those responsible state the reason? It is obvious!

**P. W. J. MACKENZIE**

*Dover Express and East Kent News*
July 3, 1913

### A SOAKING

SIR — I understand that the Folkestone
Amusements Association again have to show a
large deficit this year. In 1911 the 'extreme heat'
was to blame! Last year it was the wet summer.
But what is the excuse for this year? Can we say
it has been too wet, too hot, or is it a mixture of
the two?

Folkestone still has numerous visitors, and what
have we for them? There are hundreds of visitors
walking on the Leas with nothing whatever for
their amusement. Mr Cooper's excellent little
band of seven has to provide music for all these
people. This time two years ago Folkestone
Amusements Association allowed him sixteen
performers. Why not the same this year?

The answer is ready to hand. We are paying for
foreign labour in the shape of Herr Wurm and
his band, at the rate of from £130 to £135 per
week during the Season, and there is no money
left.

**C. STANFIELD**

*Folkestone, Hythe, Sandgate, and Cheriton Herald*
October 4, 1913

## WHYS INDEED?

SIR — Is Herr Wurm's (the Blue Viennese) band suitable for playing outdoors on the Leas? Sixty per cent of the people who pay for seats to hear the band on the Leas hear half of the music that is played, unless they happen to be up quite close to the bandstand, and on the wind side? And, besides this, should there not be more popular music played and less soft classical music? After Herr Wurm's band has gone, why does Mr Cooper's band not play in the afternoons as well as mornings, and why does not this band sometimes on a hot morning venture to play on the Leas, and not in the Leas Shelter, or 'Swelter,' as this stuffy room is called?

Why are bath-chairs allowed to be drawn up on the cliff side of the band enclosure in front of people who have paid for their chairs? Do the people in those bath-chairs pay for a ticket?

Why are dogs allowed in the band enclosure? Many of them bark and quarrel with each other—to say nothing else.

Why are the canopy chairs planted out on the point of coming on to rain? Surely these chairs could be gradually put out as people want them, and they would not then get saturated with wet. There is a terrible risk in sitting on a wet chair, be it a canvas one or a cane or wooden one.

**OBSERVER**

*Folkestone, Hythe, Sandgate, and Cheriton Herald*
October 4, 1913

## HEDGE PRUDES

SIR —I am informed by a neighbour that the extinction of the railroad hedge is meditated. I thought so. I understood Bumbledom and its spirit too well to expect that it could resist the temptation to tear up any charming rustic object that remains in a borough in order to clear the way for dreary, ugly, and mean little railings. What love of the beautiful—if it be only that for the 'shrill green' budding beauty of a hawthorn hedge in spring time—is to be expected in a borough whose prurient-minded attitude towards the study of the nude in art classes deserves nothing but contempt, making itself a laughing stock wheresoever the British press penetrates.

**ROBERT O'MEARA**

*Folkestone, Hythe, Sandgate, and Cheriton Herald*
December 6, 1913

## KHYBER PASS

SIR — On leaving the Circus, Wednesday (evening performance) I stumbled with others via the New Cross Road over big stones and through mud holes in the dark to Regent Street as best I could. Now, is it not time that this road should be properly made up, and at least two lamps placed there to light up this apparently only means of

connection with the new Railway Station.
**PROGRESS**
*Whitstable Times and Tankerton Press*
July 25, 1914


## PUNCH UP

SIR — Why should the sensibilities and feelings
of so many of us who have lost our dear one in
the war be outraged and shocked by the performances of the proprietor of a puppet show so
near to the monument which embodies reverence
and respect which we show to our honoured
dead? The place for the Punch and Judy show is
near the boat-house on the Lower Road.
**GEORGE I. WILLSON**
*Folkestone, Hythe, Sandgate, and Cheriton Herald*
January 19, 1924


## FLORENTINE ROSEMARY

SIR — I should like to add my vote of protest
against the performance of Punch and Judy so
close to the War Memorial.
I was concluded that it was a sheer spirit of con-
trariness which sanctioned it. Certainly let the
children laugh—but there is a time and place.
That place is where they should be reverent, and
bare their heads in memory of 'the boys who did
not grow up,' who went down that slope, and

who never came back. I think the idea of
planting that rosemary was exquisitely beautiful.
The War Memorial is the last resting place of
many of those heroes. I have in mind particularly
two. One was shot by a sniper and buried
'somewhere near Ginchy,' grave not registered.
He was my brother, and I have the sad pride of
laying flowers in his memory, and shedding a tear
for his widow and three children, and his brother,
none of whom are here. Another, a boy of
eighteen years, 'a nice boy,' just joined up as a
motor driver, soon afterwards 'blown to pieces.'
What does that Memorial mean to his mother?

**FLORENTINE**

*Folkestone, Hythe, Sandgate, and Cheriton Herald*
January 19, 1924

## PUNCHED OUT

SIR —I enclose for your information a copy of a
petition by residents living in the vicinity of the
Leas praying for relief from the nuisance of
Punch's penetrating voice every day and all day
long in the summer season. Most people will
probably agree with the Mayor, who, at the last
meeting of the Council, expressed the view that
the continual performance must be a nuisance to
people living near. It is indeed so!

**GEO. MACEY**

*Folkestone, Hythe, Sandgate, and Cheriton Herald*
February 2, 1924

## SLOW POKES

SIR — I think the sooner the managers of the East Kent Railway discard their old engine, the 'Walton Park,' and put on the line an engine that can do the journey and up to time, the better it will be for all concerned. A month ago it missed the connection with the main line at Shepherdswell, and passengers to Dover had to wait an hour for the next train; on the return journey, with a struggle, it crawled to Wingham an hour and a quarter late, and above all, passengers to Wingham were invited to walk from Staple by the engine driver as he could not keep up his steam.

**A SUPPORTER OF THE LOCAL LINE**
*Dover Express and East Kent News*
October 23, 1925

## MORONS

SIR — It was somewhat surprising to read in your last issue a letter signed 'Resident,' advocating cement blocks in place of our old-world picturesque footpaths that with proper attention are as easily kept in order as are the ugly modern substitutes. I have never heard that any resident in Eastbourne has wished for their red brick footpaths to be 'scrapped,' but I have heard that Eastbourne has a sobriquet of 'Stupid Sussex.'

**ANOTHER RESIDENT**

*Kent & Sussex Courier*
October 16, 1925

## CHILD ABUSE

SIR — I would esteem it a great favour if you would, out of fairness to my child, aged 14, allow me, through the columns of your paper, to contradict the ruthless rumour circulated by thoughtless people as to her.

**ROLAND ECKHOFF**

*Dover Express and East Kent News*
March 28, 1930

## MOTOR GRUDGE

SIR — I am told that Kent is proud of its roads. Kent may have cause, I do not know—I am not a motorist. But what of Kent's footpaths? No cause for pride there, at least round St. Margaret's—grit, stones, puddles, chalk, mud!

**NEW COMER**

*Dover Express and East Kent News*
February 2, 1934

## SORE THUMB

SIR — What might have been a very serious accident occurred to me on Saturday last. Considering the crowded state of the footpaths, with the large number of children free of school duties, it is marvellous that no more casualties took place. The facts are as follows:—About 11.45 am, just outside Cannon Street, a horsed van, whose driver was delivering goods, was standing alongside the footpath, and in front a baker's hand truck. The horse had a muzzle on his head, and as I was passing along he began rubbing his nose against the shaft of the truck nearest the centre of the road, it became entangled in the pronged leather straps of the muzzle. In freeing himself he took fright, raising his head which caused the bread truck to be upset, throwing the contents on to my left arm, injuring my thumb and wrist, and damaging my coat sleeves.

**ARTHUR C. HILLS**
*Dover Express and East Kent News*
July 28, 1916

## SAHARAN DRAFTS

SIR — Recently, on a brilliant, warm, sun-shiny day, I travelled in a red bus with only one of the side windows and the small one at the front open. In warm weather, every window in the bus should be down, especially those at the back. The result of having the back of the vehicle close in is that it makes a screen against which the air rebounds, so that, instead of having the wind in one's face, it is at the back of one's neck.

This is specially noticeable in cold weather, when only the ventilators are open. I have often seen people hitching up their collars and furs to protect them from the draught behind. If the back were always open, winter and summer, the buses would be much more comfortable. In reality, the red buses are wrongly constructed. The entrance should be at the back instead of at the side.

**A CONSTANT PASSENGER**
*Folkestone, Hythe, Sandgate, and Cheriton Herald*
October 19, 1915

**POINTLESS CHANGE**

## TOFF CHARITY

SIR — Fully agreeing with 'One of the People', it struck me that some additional remarks might be made to the purpose, upon the principle enunciated by Lord Palmerston. As to discussion in the House of Commons, he found that a number of speakers hammering away upon the same subject, although their arguments may be very similar, will produce more effect than the most elaborate speech by one.

As originally constituted funds were sufficient for the school being free, but owing to the alienation of property, and the relative depreciation in value of that which remained it can no longer be so. The Corporation, if faithful to their trust, should provide as good and as cheap an education as possible for the children of needy persons.

The climax, in the latest discussion appears to have been reached by the Town Clerk (although by what right he addresses the Council upon general subjects I am puzzled to imagine) who is reported to have said that if the terms were lowered, the present class of boys would leave, and a lower order be substituted.

Should such be the case, no great wrong would be inflicted, as the institution was originally founded for the children of needy persons. Before the subject was broached in the Town Council you were loud in your denunciations, since then not a word has appeared on the subject.

**A NEEDY PERSON**

*Maidstone Telegraph*
September 3, 1861

## GRATUITOUS TERGIVISATORS

SIR — I have no more faith in newspaper principles than I have in the professions of municipal or parliamentary candidates.

On August 24, a writer alluded to the usurpation of his office by the Town Clerk in the recent discussions on the Grammar School, but while making this gratuitous charge he failed to state how? The Town Clerk gave it as his simple opinion that the contemplated reduction of the school charge would be injurious to the efficiency of the school, and what man in the Council is more capable of giving opinion on this subject?

I cannot, for the life of me, see the tergiversation in a man changing his opinion, however pledged to opposite views he might have been previously.

I have carefully read the report on the Grammar school, and do not find a single argument to influence me in altering my opinion that all change is not improvement. As the school is now most efficiently conducted it would be better to leave well alone. I do not find in that report one fact to warrant that the school was ever entirely free, or exclusively for the sons of needy men.

**A CONSERVATIVE**
*Maidstone Telegraph, Malling Chronicle, and West Kent Messenger*
September 7, 1861

\*\*\*

## EXGASPERATION

SIR — I have just received my gas account for the quarter ending December, and am most disagreeably astounded at its contents, never having been charged such an amount before. Is there any satisfaction in having our gas charged 1s 6d per 1,000 less, if we are to have that of an inferior quality? We are told that more is consumed on account of the pressure, and that the dissatisfied may see the illuminating power tested at the Gas Works. What does this mean? Is the new gas company defunct?

**J.B.**
*Kentish Gazette*
March 6, 1866

## FATAL FIRES

SIR — It seems to me that there must be want of public spirit in this place, seeing that there does not exist any precautionary means against fire whatever. An ordinary portable hose reel is needed, which could be worked by volunteers on the shortest possible notice. This could be housed in a small shed, and a man to look after and keep it in working order. The recent fire at Mickleburgh House—and a more terrible one in its fatal results some few years ago in King-street—ought to be a sufficient incentive.

**VIATOR**
*Whitstable Times and Herne Bay Herald*
June 17, 1876

## BATH RAGE

SIR — Shop assistants, except for the Wednesday early closing, have no chance of a dip or of witnessing a polo match. With an indoor bath the busiest time would be the evening. The daytime could be allotted to ladies or visitors, or local schools; but the evening, after seven o'clock, would see the bath simply crowded. Many like myself have during the past summer turned down to the local bath, after a broiling day, at eight o'clock in the evening, only to be told we are too late. It is not every assistant who can afford to tire himself out for the day by walking a mile to the Baths at five o'clock am in order to be back to breakfast at seven o'clock or 7.30 before shop opens. Very few towns of the size of Tunbridge Wells have not got a proper bath, and that this many soon

be remedied here is
**A SHOP ASSISTANT**
*Kent & Sussex Courier*
October 11, 1893


## CLEAR AS MUD

SIR — I am convinced that much more water is
wasted by turning off the supply at night than by
letting it remain on. It is turned off during the
hours no one is using it and comes on so muddy
in the morning that gallons must necessarily be
wasted until the water runs clearer, for who could
use it in its first thick, muddy condition, while if
not turned off none is wasted, so why turn it
off?
Yours very truly,
**W. G. BLANCHARD**
*Whitstable Times and Herne Bay Herald*, Saturday
May 27, 1922


## ASS BACKWARDS

SIR — We are all proud of the building erected
on the Front, particularly with its oyster dredger
mounted on top, symbolic of Whitstable. But
there is something peculiar about the boat. Is it a
coincidence only—that it is sailing with its head
to the wind?
The object of my letter is to voice the judgment

of all residents living in houses where the water is turned off from 6 pm to 6 am — a very much more needed necessity, or to put it mildly, improvement.

In view of the grave position of our water supply how beneficial to health and would be the erection of earth closets in the vicinity of all houses where the absence of water makes it a real necessity. At first thought this suggestion may be considered retrograde, but it's all a matter of design: nice little summer houses, sentry boxes, pill boxes, etc. They would be very much more modern than the conditions under which many find themselves to-day in a seaside resort, which I once read was to become in time second only to Brighton.

One who arrives too late and leaves too early, to test the waters.

**PERPLEXED**
*Whitstable Times and Herne Bay Herald*
August 19, 1922

## ELECTRIC OUTRAGE

SIR — We hear so much of the need for economy and the inability of the Council to keep the street lamps alight all night except during the winter. On two occasions recently the electric street lamps in Forrest-road and the white city estate have been alight not only all night but all day as well! Would it not be more economic to

employ a man to light and extinguish these lamps
rather than automatic switch?

**ECONOMICAL**

*Kent & Sussex Courier*
August 30, 1923

## FILTHY-RICH STOMACHS

SIR — There are still a few of the old gentry left
who will live long in the memory of the out-of-
work ex-soldier who now struggle to support a
wife and child. But unfortunately they are
passing, only to be replaced by the new rich a
large number of whom are self-made invalids
through their general over-indulgence and lack of
respects for their stomachs. They are totally
ignorant of the management of a household, yet
abuse good servants who are really of a better
class than themselves.

**A MARRIED BUTLER**

*Kent & Sussex Courier*
September 7, 1923

## SEEING BLUE

SIR — I am sure I am voicing the opinion of
many when I raise against Beauty Competitions
for girls and boys between the ages of ten and
fourteen. We spend hundreds of pounds—as we
ratepayers know—on the education of the

young, for schools, public libraries, scholarships, and clubs. Men and women give up hours of their lives for helping in this most necessary and valuable work, and yet apparently encourage these most senseless competitions.

Can anyone really think that such competitions tend to help towards the uplifting of character or healthy recreation for either boy or girl? Beauty is a gift like any other given to mankind, and competition is excellent in its own way as an incentive for further effort, but can competitions for this nature for the youth of to-day help our boys to become manly or our girls to remain modest?

As for the competition for the 'most handsome lady over thirty,' I am amazed to think that any woman over that age has time to-day to think of such a thing.

**LADY NINA COHEN**
*Folkestone, Hythe, Sandgate, and Cheriton Herald*
August 23, 1924

## POLICE-COURT GAUNTLET

SIR — Now that good music has come to be widely welcomed as an aid to citizenship in its fullest sense, it seems to me that those who control our Public Libraries might do well to examine the practicability of setting apart rooms where the best music could be rendered free by gramophone.

Yesterday the gramophone was a toy, and a somewhat unpleasant one at that; to-day there is not a true music lover who fails to treasure it. Already, I am told, as many as 65,000 people have attended the really high-class gramophone concerts which are being given at Wembley— surely a phenomenal symptom of a remarkable public craving. Where the demand is so widespread and so sound it does seem strange that thousands to whom tenth-rate fiction is available on demand should be shut out from enjoying the great creators of melody and masterly interpreters of their work like Kreisler, Heifetz, Galli-Curei, and Caruso.

Make the gramophone room sound-proof. It that were done, one could avoid the risk of a Beethoven symphony disturbing the students of the latest police-court news.

**PATRICK COLLINS**

*Folkestone, Hythe, Sandgate, and Cheriton Herald*
September 6, 1924

## CABIN ANGST

SIR — While appreciating the excellent service of omnibuses which we enjoy, especially the comfortable red buses, one feels constrained to ask, in the case of the new type with the isolated driver's 'cabin,' what would happen if the driver were suddenly taken ill or other accident occurred on Sandgate-hill or other dangerous section of the route? Would the conductor be able to take control of the bus, or is there any auxiliary brake which could be applied from the body of the car? An accident might be checked by some means of dual control, which to those versed in necessary technical knowledge, should, one thinks, be a simple proposition to devise.

**G. OBEAU**

*Folkestone, Hythe, Sandgate, and Cheriton Herald*
October 11, 1924

## COUNCIL FASCISTS

SIR — Everyone knows the road from Bidborough Corner to Penshurst. Inspired with Fascist slogan of 'Speed and Destruction', the members of the Council are converting this important high road into a racing track for motorists. The beeches are being felled, the green hedges replaced by hurdles, and the primrose banks by splodges of yellow mud.

**A PROGRESSIVE**

*Kent & Sussex Courier*
May 15, 1925

## SCANDAL LADS

SIR — There is too much time wasted during school hours upon subjects which prove little benefit to those who will henceforth have to earn their daily bread. I am told that swimming, cricket and football come under the heading of PE. There is abundance of time for recreation when schools are closed. The nature of my calling brings me closely in touch with lads who have just left school, and they cannot read. Even the pronunciation of type-written words is simply astounding.

**AN OLD BOY**
*Kent & Sussex Courier*
July 17, 1925

## VOTES UP IN THE AIR

SIR — Alderman H. J. Willmot stated that the Council had decided that wireless aerials over public highways were dangerous, and that the owners of the same are to be instructed to have them removed.

No doubt the Council have gone thoroughly into the dangers of these aerials, and before deciding to enforce the new Act have obtained statistics as to the number of accidents caused through aerials falling into public highways.

There are approximately 3,000 holders of wireless receiving licenses in this borough (and these are increasing every week) and I should say that an estimate of 10,000 burgesses who are interested in wireless broadcasting would be on the low side, and taking these together with their neighbours who, though not possessing wireless sets, have kindly allowed aerials to be fixed to their chimneys, and persons who cannot afford a wireless set, but are grateful for the opportunity to 'listen in,' I think one would find that they constituted a majority of the electorate, and could safely be said to have raised no objection to aerials crossing the public highways.

**TRANSFORMER**
*Kent & Sussex Courier*
October 16, 1925

## CUTTING-OFF CHEEK

SIR — We who live in the neighbourhood of Albert Rd, would be most grateful if you would ask someone who had lately had a wireless set installed to have it looked to, for he is causing great interference, sometimes cutting others off altogether, and making it quite difficult to hear.

**A SUFFERER**
*Dover Express and East Kent News*
24 August, 1928

## TOO CLOSE FOR COMFORT

SIR — If pylons disfigure our countryside, what can one say about those hideous black monsters which stare us in the face at every turn in our borough, which is supposed to pride itself on its tidy appearance? I am referring to telegraph or telephone poles if you like. They are undoubtedly necessary evils, but surely for goodness sake some care should be taken as to where they are placed. We find them dumped down at our very doorstep and at the edge of the pavement, too, a danger to pedestrians on a dark night. If it was necessary to extend the telephone service in this locality, I should have thought the poles could have been placed in a less conspicuous position.

**DISGUSTED**

*Kent & Sussex Courier*
January 29, 1932

## BBC ROT

SIR — As one who has followed the correspondence on radio programmes with keen interest, may I express the hope that your correspondents resist the temptation to make this a Sabbatarian question. The appeal of the advertising stations is not confined to Sundays. Foreign programmes appeal to me every day of the week. And while the Sabbatarians may throw out their cheap jibes about 'vocal minorities' (ye gods!) the fact remains that many thousands of people daily ignore the BBC programmes and tune in to the sponsored programmes. After all, when so

many of our fellow countrymen do that,
surely something is seriously wrong?
**ATLAS**
*Kent Messenger*
January 29, 1938


## HORDES BRACING

SIR — Being a person who appreciated the
variety on Sundays from 12.30 onwards on
national or regional programmes, I should like
to support in a general way the letter of
'Listener' Boughton Monchelsea, more
especially his words 'the BBC must not be
stampeded by an extremely vocal minority,'
etc. In my view, as an ordinary listener, the
BBC succeed in the musical part quite well.
Take for instance last Sunday: a band with
cello player; then a fine quintet whose music
is always nice for the unlearned like myself;
then gardening; oratorio; then a mixture of
religion and music and so on. Carry on BBC!
**FREDERICK D. WELCH**
*Kent Messenger*
January 29, 1938


## CONCRETE LUMPS

SIR — I note that the Borough Council has
developed a determination to make Tunbridge

Wells a Mecca for visitors. For argument's
sake, let us suppose the Council is successful.
Some bright person will undoubtedly come
along and erect a monstrous hotel out of
concrete so the present hotel owners will see
their establishments spurned as being old-
fashioned.

**P. ELSLEY**
February 19, 1939

# FEMALE FRIGHT

## PUSSIES

SIR — Allow me to ask why are you so silent
with regards to the movement now going on in
America in favour of the rights of woman? Is
she not of sufficient worth in your estimation to
notice the struggle of the transatlantic fair for
the enfranchisement of their sex? If ladies aspire
to be senators in America, why not in Old
England? Ladies could not out-talk, for that, sir,
is the common by unfounded charge made by
your (the rougher sex) against us; but we could
not out-talk your parish boards, according to
your own reports, no, nor the House of
Commons. Now, sir, had you elected me, the
members of that house, presuming that they are
gentlemen, could not refuse a *seat* to me.
P.S. You shall hear again from us at greater
length.
**A LADY**
*West Kent Guardian*
July 12, 1851

## WOMEN MENACE

SIR — May I point out to your middle-class
women readers the urgent necessity for voting on
Tuesday next. The working woman will use her
vote – be sure of that – and if we do not
exercise our franchise we shall find the Council

dominated by Socialists who will run our rates up.

**A WOMAN RATEPAYER**

*Kent & Sussex Courier*

October 28, 1921

\*\*\*

## TROLLOPS

SIR — As a father of five boys, I should like to protest against the modern immodest garb with which some mothers deck their dear little girls – some considerably over ten – to the disgust of the community. All this piffle about the 'golden girl' and 'irresistible Eve' must make the devil smile. 'Man traps' would be a better name for some of them.

**FREDERICK C. GLASS**

*Kent & Sussex Courier*

August 24, 1923

## STOCKING FEAR

SIR — What a legacy of rheumatism is being stored up by the ridiculous fashion of wearing thin transparent stockings which are making drapers' fortunes! I hope that Tunbridge Wells will remain dowdy.

**MATRON**

*Kent & Sussex Courier*

August 31, 1923

## MAID TO WEAR

SIR — Whoever heard of maids taking their mistresses' blouses to wear except in books? As regards to apeing our mistresses – well surely we maids can follow the fashions without being accused of apeing. We earn an honest living, and should be allowed to spend our money as we wish.

**DISGUSTED DOMESTIC**
*Kent & Sussex Courier*
September 7, 1923

## ANKLE FINGER

SIR — All this fuss about girls showing their necks or arms or ankles is perfectly ridiculous. It may not suit the old tabbies who go to awfully Low Churches in this narrow-minded town, but I am glad to see even dancing is trying to establish itself, however much it is frowned upon.

**GIRL OF THE PERIOD**
*Kent & Sussex Courier*
September 7, 1923

## WEARING TROUSERS

SIR — Suppose we wrote concerning a man's dress to your paper, do you think any men would take notice? Then, why should we?

**16 YEAR OLD**
*Kent & Sussex Courier*
September 21, 1923

\*\*\*

### NOT A SHRINKING VIOLET

SIR — I would like to answer the letter in your paper last week. All the girls I know are quite capable of making intelligent conversation but the majority of our young possess one-track minds, that is, cricket in the summer, football in the winter. If the days are past when it was a matter of necessity for a man to pay the expenses of the opposite sex, so also is the time when a woman's chief aim was to charm.
**PANSY RATCLIFF**
*Kent & Sussex Courier*
September 15, 1933

### GENDER BENDERS

SIR — For the benefit of the travelling public, do you think that you could obtain the East Kent Road Car Company's definition of 'workman'? Must he be dressed in overalls and generally covered in dust to be able to travel on a workman's bus at a workman's fare? If so, women are barred.
**T. T.**
*Dover Express and East Kent News*
March 5, 1937

**HAVE FAITH**

## A PURPLE TSUNAMI

SIR — I cannot but view with suspicion, the unprecedented march of Popery in our country. The Catholics themselves calculate, at the least, that they have an accession of 2,000 annually to their ranks from the Protestant Church. Protestants have been supine, negligent, and indifferent. How many there are calling themselves churchmen, and yet are, in their conduct and deportment worse than Infidels.

**C. G.**

*West Kent Guardian*
March 2, 1839

## PARTY PAUPERS

SIR — 'The Working Classes are invited to attend.' Such were the words appended to a notice announcing a service to be held at St. Paul's Church, on the day of its consecration. I would ask, was the treatment of them such as would induce them to go? I think not. Not having 'tickets' most of them were excluded. Amongst the number were several who had assisted by their honest labour in rearing the structure. The labouring population were told in the evening by the Incumbent that the church was built specially for their benefit. If that be so, how came it to pass that they were not 'specially' invited.

**A CHURCHMAN**

*Maidstone Telegraph, Rochester and Chatham Gazette* January 19, 1861

## BAPTISM OUTRAGE

SIR — Will you permit me to ask whether any of your readers could supply information respecting a wide-spread rumour that a poor woman, residing in Scrubb's Lane, has been refused relief in consequence of her child not having been Christened?

[We have heard a rumour of the above, but can scarcely give credence that such a gross outrage upon humanity could be perpetrated. If any of our readers have any facts to communicate in reference thereto, we shall be glad to expose the transaction or deny it.—Ed.]

**INQUIRER**

*Maidstone Telegraph, Rochester and Chatham Gazette,* February 9, 1861

## UNSUITABLE SOULS

SIR — From the wife of a clergyman of the Church of England: 'a housemaid who thoroughly understands her duties and can wait at a table. *No one from Maidstone will suit.*' Such a wholesale implication of ability is contrary to the general characteristics of the servants of Maidstone. They have another trait: that of knowing the value of their labour and the lack of that docility which characterises those born in the agricultural districts. I am aware clerical arrogance is wont to rule supreme of all in agricultural villages, where the poor dare not call their souls their own.

**THE FIRST STONE**

*Maidstone Telegraph, Rochester and Chatham Gazette*
April 27, 1861

## UNHOLY CARRY ON

SIR —Yesterday (Sunday) a sad and most unbecoming proceeding occurred in Broomfield Chapel, Herne. After the evening service on Sunday a gang from the Bay, who had previously conducted the service, demanded the key, and as the key was refused, a most abominable affair ensued. Rev. Mr Blandford, Mr Sands, and another were confined to the chapel until 10 o'clock, singing and abusive threatening being carried on, and Mr Sands was threatened by three different persons' clenched fists in his attempt to escape. The meeting was only dispersed by the key of the chapel being reluctantly given up.

**AN EYEWITNESS**

*Whitstable Times and Herne Bay Herald*
February 1, 1879

## RINGING TRIBUTE

SIR — On Sunday, in two hours 38 minutes a peal of Grandsire Doubles, 5,040 changes, was run on the bells of Eythorne Church. The ringers were our own, two of the weaker sex, Joyce Bean, who was 15 that day, and Mrs Chivers, the mother for four children. I contend that this peal constitutes a record for Kent.

**J.W. HORSLEY**
*Kent Messenger*
January 1, 1938

## ZZZZZZ

SIR — The Feast which commemorates the passing of the Mother of Our Lord is one which no Anglican would willingly ignore. The belief that she died in the ordinary way rests, of course, upon a historical foundation. The belief, however, that she was raised again from the dead and transmitted to Heaven and there crowned as Queen of the Heavenly Court rests upon no foundation whatever. As a matter of fact, the departed were, in the earliest age of the Church, conceived of as being in Paradise. There is something highly unsatisfactory about the Feast's title: 'The Assumption'. Would it not be best for us Anglicans to use exclusively the title known in

71

the orthodox East: 'The Falling-Asleep'?
**LEWIS INNES**
*Folkestone, Hythe, Sandgate, and Cheriton Herald*
August 23, 1924


## PIOUS PIFFLE

SIR — In the days of the dodo, people kept the Sabbath and anything else they could lay their hands upon. In these strenuous days the great thing to keep is to keep fit, and as an aid to cheerfulness the Sunday cinema has been an asset to this end to many thousands. Moreover, what would have been said if some of us suggested the closing of churches because they sometimes encourage gloom and ill-feeling? As much pious piffle has been talked by our representatives on the Town Council, it would be just as well to elect in future aspirants with more rational views.
**H. P. TARRANT**
*Dover Express and East Kent News*
November 7, 1930


## MILK DEVILS

SIR — Many residents demand the milkman calling twice on Sunday. On occasions he has been told: 'We won't want any more milk, but will you send back some cream in time for lunch?' Three parts of the people who require two deliveries on Sundays are churchgoers.

**DISGUSTED MILKMAN**
*Kent & Sussex Courier*
February 6, 1931

## SUNDAY BLINKERS

SIR — I have heard and read many strong protests against Sunday amusements, but I have yet to hear a sermon against Sunday labour. But the commandment reads: 'in it thou shalt do no manner of work, thou, nor thy servant.'

**MARK ANDREW**
*Kent & Sussex Courier*
February 13, 1931

## ABSOLUTELY CHRISTIAN

SIR — Since when have politics anything to do with religion? If we had more Christianity in the world we should need less politics.

**RAMOND G. MEDHURST**
*Kent & Sussex Courier*
November 20, 1936

## RELIGIOUS RACKET

SIR — The refusal of the request by petitioners

to place the *Daily Worker* in the newspaper room at the Public Library is typical of Dovorian officialdom. Nonetheless, the management of the Library are gifted with a sense of humour. One sees a printed notice when entering, 'Silence is requested.'

You sit down whilst close to you Mrs Brown is in animated conversation with Mrs Smith, their topic being the affairs of Mrs White. Borrowers are tramping from shelf to shelf wearing iron-shod clogs. A child is racing from one end of the room to the other, giving lungs full play. On top of all this the telephone bell rings, loud as any fire alarm. Out in the lobby some baby is yelling for its mother who is inside selecting another book.

Someday we may have built for us a Public Library conforming with the latest civilised ideas that is, bomb-proof and gas-proof, and if then we are allowed to read what we like there may be a more cosmopolitan variety of literature — material to this world, not the next, as is so much in evidence on the tables of the present newspaper room.

**PRO BONO PUBLICIO**
*Dover Express and East Kent News*
September 24, 1937

**CHRIST ON CREMATION**
SIR — I am struck by the puerility of the

arguments of the anti-cremationists. For instance, a lady last week asserts that cremation is contrary to Christianity. Where is the evidence that Christ ever expressed himself on the subject?

**F. RIDLINGTON**
*Kent & Sussex Courier*
January 28, 1938

\*\*\*

## FURY OF THE LORD

SIR — How fully is Scripture being fulfilled in the air raid preparations: 'They shall go into the holes of the rocks and into the caves of the earth for fear of the Lord' (Isaiah): 'The great men, the rich man and kings of the earth hid themselves in the dens and in the rocks of the mountains and said hide us from the face of him that sitteth on the throne' (Revelations).

**M. E. WELLDON**
*Kent & Sussex Courier*
April 14, 1939

## ARMAGEDDON MUDDLE?

SIR — I find this [above] letter a trifle perplexing. We hear so many rumours in these rapidly changing times, but I, and I am sure many others, are under the impression that we are have been preparing shelters as a protection against attacks by Hitler and Mussolini, not, as your correspondent suggests, to escape the fury of the Lord.

**M. H.**
*Kent & Sussex Courier*
April 21, 1939

**GREAT PEEVES**

## GERM-FREE

SIR — I should feel very much obliged if you
would be kind enough to contradict in *The
Whitstable Times* the rumour that is being
circulated in the town that I am a German.
My father was a native of Oxfordshire and my
mother was a Kentish woman.
German labour is very much employed in my
trade, but I have never employed any, or likely to.
**H. G. SURMAN**
*Whitstable Times and Tankerton Press*
August 29, 1914

## CLIFF HANGER

SIR — Will you kindly insert in your paper the
information that the footpath to Shakespeare
Cliff, and road leading from the town, is quite
open and free to visitors. Since the war
commenced there has been a great falling off of
visitors coming to our famous cliff, and I have
been informed that they are under the impression
that the path to the cliff is 'closed to the public'.
I can assure them such is not the case. I can
speak from experience, as I live that way myself.
To be on holiday to Dover and leave the town
without seeing the view from the cliff is a great
loss, for I think it most splendid myself. People

would be challenged by the sentries after dark, no doubt, but we all know there could be no view after dark.

[We find that this is so. It is, however, advisable not to proceed beyond the top of Shakespeare Cliff.—Ed.]

**SHAKESPEARE**
*Dover Express and East Kent News*
August 28, 1914


## FIRM ROT

SIR — Some firms are granting the men half-pay during the time they are serving, others I am sorry to say will not even keep open one's situation. This sort of rottenness can be overcome if employers grant that situations will remain open. A tour of shops would do good to find out what people are helping the enemy.

**PRISONER**
*Dover Express and East Kent News*
September 4, 1914


## TREAT ROCKET

SIR — It is not realised what an unkindness it is in public houses to 'treat' those who, without this mistaken kindness, would be more alert to serve their King and country. The real way to serve the country in time of war is for our town to set an

example by closing them from 9 pm to 9 am
daily, and on Sunday entirely.
**R. B. CAY**
*Dover Express and East Kent News*
September 4, 1914

### LIGHTWEIGHT TUNBRIDGE WELLS

SIR — In Tunbridge Wells on Saturday
afternoon, a gentleman of middle-age was
speaking to a young shopman of about 23: 'No,
I'm not going. They won't catch me (A cynical
giggle). I don't want to be shot. Besides, if they
want men of our class they ought to offer more.
Why, just look at how they feed them. I'm told
the food they get is awful! Just bread and butter
for breakfast!' He sniggered.
The gentleman urged that many, many were
wanted; that the time might come when men
would be forced to serve through conscription.
'Oh, no!' exclaimed this young citizen. 'There's
no need of that! We've got plenty of men out
there, and they're sending some more out.' At
this I spoke out. 'So you won't enlist because you
can't have your eggs and bacon for breakfast!' I
said, 'And what are you and creatures like you
going to do when the men who are being
butchered, perhaps at this moment?' He said it
wasn't my business to interfere.
I told him that every man in my own family was
in the army; that my husband had two brothers, a

gunner and a sailor; and that my poor old servant goes in daily anguish for her two sons in the thick of the most dreadful battle the world has known.

It seems that in Tunbridge Wells few in proportion to the population have come forward at this moment of life and death.

**ISABEL KENNEDY, nr Tonbridge**

*Kent & Sussex Courier*
September 4, 1914


## SPINELESS BIRDS

SIR — There is apparently someone residing near Kearsney who has taken upon herself the task of distributing white feathers to those men who she thinks are shirking the duty they owe to the country.

If it is such a commendable thing to do, whoever it is, I think she might have the courage to do so openly, and not anonymously, and it would be just as well, perhaps, if they were to find out beforehand whether the supposedly weak-hearted ones to whom she sent the feathers had offered themselves for service any way.

**E. McGRATH.**

*Dover Express and East Kent News*
September 11, 1914

## WHO'S THE DADDY?

SIR — I help entertain the soldiers at the
pavilion in the St John's Recreation Ground on
Sunday. I should like to contradict the statement
that the song You're the Sweetest Baby I Know
was sung. The song Bring Back My Daddy to Me
was sung, but surely no one would object to such
beautiful words? We do our best to compensate
our soldiers a little for all they are doing for us.
**S. E.**
*Kent & Sussex Courier*
December 18, 1914

\*\*\*

## DARKNESS CRAZE

SIR — There is reason in all things fails
absolutely in the action of our Council throwing
the town into total darkness: I and many others
can see no sense or reason in endangering life
and limb to this idiotic craze. Myself and family
with a few friends went to the entertainment at
the Church House more to support the funds
that for amusement. I was nearly knocked down
by a gentleman from the opposite direction, my
son knocked against someone else, while one
poor woman we saw actually in the mud. The
wonder is inhabitants don't unanimously protest
against such wanton childish feebleness.
**J. M. B.**
*Whitstable Times and Tankerton Press*
January 23, 1915

## FIFTH COLUMNIST

SIR — I was grieved to read JMB's letter in your last week's issue. JMB, surely, cannot be a native but must be an alien — a 'Germ-Hun'? He points out that although he saw a poor woman in the mud, he did not offer her a helping hand.

I should like to point out the inaccuracies of your correspondent. It was on the order of the Admiralty that the Council had to stop lighting the town. Situated as Whitstable is, it is absolutely essential not to have lights showing which would guide our enemy to vital points of our national defences.

I also wonder if JMB has ever troubled to ascertain the work the special constables are doing. I can assure him that doing patrol duty on a cold, windy, and raining night, watching the homes of JMB and others, is not child's play, even though we do not tumble about as he seems to in the dark.

The best advice I can give him is to stay at home out of harm's way, and to send his subscription to the funds he mentions — especially as he 'did not go to the entertainment for amusement'.

**A SPECIAL CONSTABLE**

*Whitstable Times and Tankerton Press*
January 23, 1915

## ZEPPELIN LAMP

SIR — When your correspondent JMB made his withering charge of 'childish feeble-mindedness' against our fairly young Council he surely did so forgetting that he might get one back on his own head.

One Councillor remarked at a meeting this week, 'supposing the Admiralty suggestions had not been carried out and some bombs had been dropped here, the Council would feel very sick.' This remark has been sadly supported in the case of the Yarmouth Zeppelin raid of today, 19 January, 'when the authorities after the raid ordered the street lights to be extinguished.' That was at 8.30 pm.

Have we not all tripped against curbs, trodden in muddy pools, and even 'bashed' into elderly strangers not agile enough to avoid us? First, it is a discipline, nonetheless, aimed to prepare us for martial law, which will be darker still. Second, it is a trial of skill and patience, and learning to grope about is better than living in a cellar for week as thousands of our poor friends the Belgians have had to do.

When walking on footpaths always keep to the right, and carry a pocket lamp.

**C. R. CHAMBERLAINE**
*Whitstable Times and Tankerton Press*
January 23, 1915

\*\*\*

## TRAM HAMMER

SIR — I have read with interest a letter in your columns dealing with our trams. Every word he writes is true. For years I have been hammering away at Dover Trams. Ratepayers are pouring out thousands of pounds upon a system fit only to grace the scrap heap.

**RATEPAYER**

*Dover Express and East Kent News*
August 27, 1915

## THE ORDER OF FILTH

SIR — Could anything be more revolting to the senses than the order in respect to the collection of rubbish? It would appear that the men of the new – and totally unnecessary (£1000 each) – motor cars have orders to collect nothing which is not placed either on the public way or just within a private gate; and we now have the disgusting spectacle of hundreds of fly-covered disease-traps lining all the better roads of the town. I am not concerned with why's and wherefore's and see only, with a large number of others, that it is a procedure that can only be described as filthy. Imagine such an arrangement at any self-respecting town!

**A RATEPAYER**

*Dover Express and East Kent News*
August 27, 1915

## DRUGGED HUNS

SIR —With reference to a letter in your last
week's column, signed 'J. Smith Clough,' I am
entirely in agreement with him only that we
should have appeared very foolish had we started
an Anti-Boer Union during the Boer War. Our
gallant Dutch foes waged war like high-bred
gentlemen compared with the brutal methods of
the Hun; likewise, the Boer neither menaced this
country nor our fleet, our liberty, nor our
commerce, nor did they murder helpless women
and children on land and sea. General Botha has
publicly expressed his withering contempt for
pro-Germans.

The 'cultured' Germans' poisoning of wells, and
other methods of demonstrating their system of
warfare, has probably influenced this brave Boer
general's opinion. Your columnist gives no date
as to when the 'unclean devils' possessing his
Prussian acquaintances just now may reasonably
be expected to be cast out, leaving the German
nation—so he assures us— 're-clothed and in its
right mind.' I think we can hardly be expected to
sit down any longer to await this desirable
miracle. Does your correspondent actually flatter
himself that any true or decent Briton desires any
further 'international' dealings with a nation—
lunatic, or no lunatic—who had defiantly broken
every principle of humanity in their abominable

and savage conduct of this war, and who are despised by every civilised nation?

The German 'ideals' are wanton brutality and universal world power by studied means of 'frightfulness'. God forbid we should ever possess any 'idealism' in common with these Scarborough raiders, or the dastardly sinkers of the Lusitania, or the gas poisoners of our soldiers. If we forget these crimes while our lives last, then, and then only, shall we sink to the level of the Hun.

As no man can serve two masters, we should like to see all pro-Germans, take up their permanent residence in the Fatherland at the same time, where they can indulge their 'ideals' to their hearts' content. All these persons would be better, and more comfortable surely, out of England.

Your columnist informs us that the German people have been 'horribly drugged and duped.' He is mistaken, or else misleading accounts from Berlin have reached him. It is we British who, like the fools we have been, allowed ourselves to be sweetly lulled by the false warblings of those who sang of the Kaiser's love of peace. The Hun Chancellor—Bethmann Hollweg—hardly spoke like a man asleep, when, a few days ago, he roared out his violent execrations against this country in the Reichstag, to an admiring audience.

Many persons—even of English birth—are trying to whitewash Germany in this town.

Probably several of these people belong to the 'lukewarm' order—the neither cold nor hot—to whom the voice of Revelation said: 'I will spue thee out of my mouth.'

**MEMBER OF THE ANTI-GERMAN LEAGUE**

*Folkestone, Hythe, Sandgate, and Cheriton Herald*
August 28, 1915


## ROAD ROT

Last Saturday was one of the warmest and brightest days this summer. The streets are always sufficiently dirty and insanitary; but under the present arrangement, when loose papers, cabbage leaves, entrails of fish and fowl are left on the open roadway uncollected, what is to be expected? A great improvement the Town Council will say.

**F. ROAD**

*Dover Express and East Kent News*
September 3, 1915


## GERMAN GENES

SIR — I have been away from home for about a fortnight, and on my return see there has been what one may call a virulent correspondence attacking the Anti-German Union. I venture to point out that there are ample reasons for the

88

formation of such a Union.

Germany, for the last thirty or forty years, though ostensibly friendly, has been secretly preparing to destroy the British Empire; not only that, but to obtain possession of the whole world, and, so far as we can understand, the ambition of the Kaiser was to be 'the representative of the Almighty as the ruler of the world.'

But we are still more justified when the attempt at such dominion has been attended by organized frightfulness, the murder of non-combatant men, women and children, the sinking of ships without warning, the violation of women and the mutilation of children, the wanton destruction in the countries they have been able temporarily to overrun, the breaking of treaties, and the ruthless ignoring of every rule of civilized warfare, the preaching of hate of this country even in their schools. Such acts can never be forgotten or forgiven.

The Germans were once before expelled from this country by Queen Elizabeth, and they must be so again. I would propose a prohibitive tax upon any German in the country, and double tax on anyone who employs one. Naturalization is impossible, for how can a German become a naturalised Englishman when his own country by law will not denaturalize him. Once a German, always a German.

**M. TWEEDLIE**

*Folkestone, Hythe, Sandgate, and Cheriton Herald,*
October 9, 1915

## YELL COWARDS

SIR — Thursday between 10 o'clock and noon
we had, within fifty yards of the house, a fruit
cart (fifteen yells), rags and bottles (eighteen), van
of basket-chairs (twelve), lamp and oil (six),
nondescript, probably carrots (eighteen). All
these were within thirty yards of a notice board,
and each offender passed within six feet of at
least one board. One vendor stopped and read it.
Requests for silence owing to illness are ignored,
and a hawker twice reported to the police and
repeatedly threatened tells me that the police will
not touch him. Our house is almost useless in a
morning. Everyone complains, but when asked to
bear witness each person 'did not hear it'.

**A TWO YEARS' SUFFERER**
*Folkestone, Hythe, Sandgate, and Cheriton Herald*
September 11, 1915

## UNGRATEFUL SODS

SIR — Surely they be dogs-in-the-manger, those
people in Hythe who object to soldiers riding on
the bank of the Canal. I frequently walk there,
often enough the whole length without meeting
anyone. Nor can I remember that I have met
more than half a dozen. It is not a confined
space, it is easy to get out of the way, and surely
a glance at those happy faces will compensate for

the chance of a little mud, if that be the objection of individuals. Let them think how soon those faces will smile forever.

If the Council is distressed at the injured turf, let it take comfort and leave it until after the War. It will be all smooth and level long before those narrow mounds in Flanders shall be obliterated. So with those who object to the noise made by the soldiers billet on them. Let them think of the houses in France, and ask themselves who secures their own houses from a like devastation. Does it beseem those of us who live at home in safety to nag at these gallant men and to subject them to petty vexations and childish restrictions? Will it comfort us when we read the roll of honour to know that we have stinted them in their food or their comfort while living with us?

**ONLOOKER**

*Folkestone, Hythe, Sandgate, and Cheriton Herald*
December 11, 1915

\*\*\*

### RUM CHARGE

SIR — Why were soldiers given rum before a bayonet charge? It was to arouse their animal passions and make them commit acts they would not otherwise do.

**MISS S. CANDLER, The Women's Temperance Asscociation**

*Kent & Sussex Courier*
October 6, 1916

## ATROCIOUS SLUR

SIR — Miss Candler's observations have aroused widespread indignation in the town and are calculated to give the deepest pain to those who have lost their dearest and others now facing the enemy. The association should at the earliest possible moment publicly disassociate itself from the atrocious expressions of Miss Candler.

**CHARLES C. EMSON, MAYOR**
*Kent & Sussex Courier*
October 6, 1916

## DRUNKEN TIGERS

SIR — War is horrible; the great majority of our men are naturally of noble and kindly disposition and need a stimulant as the press says 'to fight like tigers', which is all I meant.

**MISS S. CANDLER, The Women's Temperance Asscociation**
*Kent & Sussex Courier*
October 6, 1916

## OFF TO THE TRENCHES

SIR — I wish people who talk like Miss Candler could have a sample of trench-life. It is a slur on

our country excusable only because from a
fanatic. [Passed by censor]
**F. BRIDGLAND, FRANCE**
*Kent & Sussex Courier*
October 13, 1916

\*\*\*

## WAILING WOMEN

SIR — It must force itself upon our minds that
out of the hundreds of women left only a small
percentage are working in canteens, the War
Supply Depot, the Hospitals or other daily war-
work. At the end of two years those who have
been working regularly for six, eight, or ten hours
a day are beginning to feel the strain. So many
women plead they are not strong enough to help.
To these I suggest: 'Try what helping people who
are sick will do for your complaints.'
**ROSS WALTER**
*Kent & Sussex Courier*
October 17, 1916

## DEATH-TRAP TREES

SIR — I was very glad to see Mr Tewson's letter.
I quite agree with him about the superfluity of
trees in the roads, shutting out air, light and
sunshine. What with forest trees in the little front
gardens overhanging the paths and trees each
side of the road, we are deprived of the air and

93

sunshine necessary to dry the paths and keep the road healthy.

**A RESIDENT OF UPPER GROSVENOR ROAD, TUNBRIDGE WELLS**
*Kent & Sussex Courier*
October 20, 1916

\*\*\*

### CAT RAGE

SIR — Having read the proposed suggestion for a cats' home in High Brooms, I wonder if you can spare space for my letter. I am of the same opinion as 'An Indignant Mother' of last week. I am a great believer in humanity of every kind, and like cats in their place, and would not have them ill-treated—far from it—but at the same time I consider that children come first. If some cat-lover has between £250 and £500 to spare for such an unnecessary thing as a home for stray cats, why cannot they direct their charity towards poor little children who need food and clothing, and boots on their feet, and erect a shelter for them whilst poor mothers go to work to keep a shelter over their heads; or even send a little towards giving our poor 'Tommies' a little treat for Christmas, who are risking their lives to protect such people as these cat-lovers?

**A DISGUSTED MOTHER OF THREE**
*Kent & Sussex Courier*
November 24, 1916

## HOUSE FLIES

SIR — No wonder you had a letter from 'An Indignant Mother' about the suggested home for stray cats. Let us hope that wherever it is started indignant neighbours will pull it down as fast as it is raised. We shall certainly lose this war unless people get better ideas. If we do lose (or do not completely win) there will be plenty of wandering human beings to care for, besides myriads of stray cats.

As for Mr Marsh, he answers himself. If cats are disease carriers they should be destroyed like house-flies, not herded in a home. I cannot believe that subscribers approve of such a wild-cat scheme.

**CANDOUR**

*Kent & Sussex Courier*
November 24, 1916

## THANKLESS FELINES

SIR — I am a lover of all animals – even cats – when they are well disciplined, although I think at their best they are selfish and ungrateful creatures. I never get more than one night in seven without being awakened two or three times every night by hideous yelling and screeching. I willingly subscribe per head for everyone taken away – alive or dead.

**A. R. W.**

*Kent & Sussex Courier*
November 24, 1916

## DRINKING MOTHERS

SIR — As voluntary rescue worker on behalf of
the unfortunate feline race, I fancied that what I
didn't know on the subject wasn't worth knowing.
I quite agree with 'An Indignant Mother' as to
the establishment of crèches. The spectacle of
numbers of young children, from a few months
to a few years of age, left outside public houses
while their working mothers are drinking is a
pitiable sight.

**EMILY C. DIXON**
*Kent & Sussex Courier*
December 1, 1916

\*\*\*

## LANDLORD SHIRKERS

SIR — Nine out of every ten landlords refuse to
let their houses on account of the family. The
one cry is 'I only let to people without a family.'
While my husband is doing his bit for his King
and Country I am trying my hardest to
accommodate my little ones decently.

**A DISGUSTED MOTHER**
*Kent & Sussex Courier*
December 1, 1916

## SPURIOUS SPELLINGS

SIR — I find that Leigh is not mentioned in Domesday Book, in Textus Roffensis the name is written as Leaga. Will some member of the Leigh Parish Council cite the authority for suggesting the spurious archaism Lyghe?
[We are informed that the proposal has the support of Lord Hollenden, Lord De L'Isle and Dudley, *et al.*—Ed.]
**ENQUIRER**
*Kent & Sussex Courier*
December 22, 1916

## CHICKEN WASTE

SIR — Several cases have come to my notice of disappointment in chicken rearing, and in each case the owners were bringing them up indoors. As many are commencing poultry keeping this year, unless chicks can from the very first run out on to the earth or very short grass it is a waste.
**V. ROBSON**
*Dover Express and East Kent News*
April 20, 1917

## WAR DRAG

SIR — It would be interesting to know whether our Government have been constructing the

Channel Tunnel, if not, why? In addition to being a wise spending of money, this tunnel would have secured a victory by this time as over 60,000 tons per 24 hours would have been sent through releasing naval help on convoys.

**A. E. TAYLOR**
*Kent & Sussex Courier*
December 28, 1917

## DREAMING ON

SIR — Several of my visitors have cleared out with an attack of nerves because the electric light cut off three nights in a week without any apparent necessity. As the apartment houses are full of people who have come to get away from the raids in London, is it really necessary to give them these continual reminders that raids are taking place the other side of the country? The Town Council will not help them to find in beautiful Tunbridge Wells a place to forget the war.

**A LARGE RATEPAYER**
*Kent & Sussex Courier*
December 28, 1917

## BEASTLY CINEMAS

SIR — I have had the annoyance of taking my children to a local cinema and having just got comfortably seated, saw a notice that owing to the electric energy failing, the exhibition would be discontinued. No money would be refunded or re-admission tickets issued. Had I gone to the opera, the performance would have been continued with subsidiary illumination. Many people think that the cutting off of electric current in Tunbridge Wells every time there is a distant air raid is carried to absurd lengths.

**DISGUSTED**

*Kent & Sussex Courier*
December 28, 1917

## FOOD FIGHT

SIR — Those who assumed that when the Food Rationing Order came into force queues would become a thing of the past were rudely awakened at Tunbridge Wells on Saturday afternoon, when there was a repetition of the scenes which almost daily taxed the powers of the local. There was a tedious wait in the pouring rain for close upon two hours, and when the entrance was opened to the public men and women pushed an elbowed for all they were worth. It was a sorry experience for many, as, drenched to the skin, they saw the last piece snapped up and went empty away.

**HOUSEHOLDER**

*Kent & Sussex Courier*
April 12, 1918

## CRYING DISGRACE

SIR — Through your paper you have in the past drawn attention to a good many things which needed to be seen to in Dover. Many of us do wish you could draw the attention of the Lighting Committee (if there is such a thing in this town) to the need of a light mid-way between in Five Post Lane. It is a disgraceful place to have to go through after the lights in the few shops just there are put under cover. To us—who have to go through—it is a constant nightmare. It is a main artery from one part of the town to another, and as it is now, is a crying disgrace. A light—one only would do—to show right down and to light up a dark entry next to the 'Liberty' Inn.

**A WOMAN WORKER**
*Dover Express and East Kent News*
November 29, 1918

## ARMY OUTRAGE

SIR — I have three Army Pay Corps soldiers billeted with me who have been badly wounded in the war. Yesterday an ambulance drove up to my door, and demanded that one of them must get up out of bed and go to the Military Hospital. Fancy a human being, ill in bed, having to obey such orders. No blanket or anything to wrap around him. Being driven in a motor ambulance on a cold day, with one end of the vehicle open, is enough to kill anyone. Had I been at home I would have defied all the powers in the world.

**G. W. HICKS**
*Dover Express and East Kent News*
November 24, 1918

## SMALL MEDAL ENVY

SIR — Allow me, as a very old resident, to support the proposal that all of us who stayed in Dover during the raids should be allowed to wear a small ribbon or medal.

**XYZ**
*Dover Express and East Kent News*
December 29, 1918

# THE COUNTRY AT LARGE

## CAT KILLERS

SIR — I went to the above meeting from motives of curiosity. I listened attentively to the remarks of Liberal candidate Captain Brinckman, who spoke like a schoolboy saying a lesson. The other speakers were far more worth listening to, for bigoted fanatics are always more amusing, though generally as brainless, as a simple blockhead.

**C. K. S.**
*Kentish Gazette*
September 15, 1868

## OUT OF TOWNERS

SIR — We have had an invasion of foreign agitators, whose object appears to be to throw discontent amongst the working men of Whitstable. The invaders, augmented by a crowd (not representative working men), paraded the streets on Friday last with considerable noise, and it is understood that efforts were made to establish a union, the flag of which was flying on Hoxton Crescent, Ludgate Hill.

**ANTI-AGITATION**
*Whitstable Times and Herne Bay Herald*
April 5, 1890

## HYTHE SCYTHE

SIR — At a recent public meeting of the National Citizens' Union Councillor Millar, of Hythe, offered to debate 'Socialism' at any place and at any time. We presume it is the Socialism of Karl Marx he advocates. If so, why does he go to Germany for his inspiration? Would he kindly explain exactly how the application of this particular brand of Socialism will benefit Hythe? If Socialism is the one panacea for all the ills we suffer from, doubtless Mr Millar will be able to quote from history successful applications of these doctrines and communities who living in a state of bliss and prosperity.

**VERITAS**

*Folkestone, Hythe, Sandgate, and Cheriton Herald*
February 9, 1924

## SOBER TRUTH

SIR — The majority of people in this country are not teetotallers. If Mr Bristow believes the public does not want cheaper and better beer, he knows very little about the public.

**B. B. WILLIAMS**

*Kent & Sussex Courier*
January 29, 1932

## RED RAGE

SIR — The Communists, backed by Russia, intend to hold an International anti-God Conference in London next April to show the growth of the movement in this country. It is unthinkable that this conference should be allowed to take place. If every village in Kent sent up a petition, signed by the residents, it would stop it.

**MRS DAPHNE DENNE**
*Kent Messenger*
January 28, 1938

## THE RED AND THE BLACK

SIR — I can never understand why the Labour Party has such a strong dislike of the Nazi government. Herr Hitler's is a Socialist form of government: the workers come first, the so-called employers are taxed right up to the hilt and are bound by all sorts of rules; titles are abolished and class distinction is claimed to have been abolished. Perhaps someone can enlighten me?

**DEMOCRAT**
*Kent & Sussex Courier*
May 5, 1939

## EMPEROR'S CLOTHES

SIR — From the cradle to the grave the life of

the worker is taxed out of all proportion to his income. Fifteen shillings out of every twenty raised in national taxation is spent on militarism to pay for capitalist wars and for holding down subject peoples. That is where the money goes. A fraction of it would provide the necessary capital to build a healthy and beautiful house for every homeless family in the country. How many Englishmen can be proud of the Empire when most of their countrymen are without the first requirements of civilised life?

**PHILIP MILLWOOD**
*Kent & Sussex Courier*
June 29, 1923


## EMPIRE DELIVERY

SIR — The great Exhibition at Wembley, a wonderful example of varied communities widely scattered but knit together by their citizenship of a common Empire, has provided a magnificent advertisement for the resources and productions of our own lands.

At the same time, the figures of unemployment have again taken an alarming upward leap, and we seem to be faced with a winter which will be unparalleled in privation and suffering for millions of British citizens. These considerations lead me to suggest that the present is an opportune time for us in Tunbridge Wells to play our part. As a start in this direction, my firm, are

arranging to hold a special 'All-British' Week. I
am personally offering a special prize of a gold
sovereign for the best explanation on a postcard
of 'Why We Should Buy British Goods.'
**F. NOAKES, Junr.**
*Kent & Sussex Courier*
October 16, 1925


## HARLOT SCARE

SIR — I see that the Rev. Claud Coffin is giving
lectures in Dover, warning us to be prepared for
a Great World Crisis. I remember the previous
warning some seven years ago which so
frightened the landladies of Weymouth, who
were to be submerged in a great tidal wave, the
precursor of Armageddon. That scare went off
as a damp squib.
As reported in your current issue, the Rev. Mr
Coffin notifies much warlike activity in the lands
controlled by Gog and Magog and among the
turbulent inhabitants of Ethiopia and Libya. We
have also to keep our eyes on Gomer. As far as I
can find out, Gomer was the unfaithful wife of a
Hebrew prophet [Hosea] who bored his spouse
to tears. Rising from her ashes she also is to
attack the British Empire [in Palestine]. What is
our National Government doing?
I have read a small book by the Regius Professor
of Divinity in the University of Oxford on the
British-Israel theory: if the British people were

indeed descended from the last Hebrew tribes a
Comparative Grammar could be compiled
showing the evolution of English from Hebrew.
Records in the British Museum Library would
soon explode any such contention.

**A. L. CALDWELL**
*Dover Express and East Kent News*
January 11, 1935

## MUSTARD GAS

SIR — If Maurice Spencer or Eric E. Leigh
think that I am swallowing the bait which they so
temptingly offered to get me to carry on with
them a lengthy correspondence as to the merits
of demerits of the League of Nations in
Musollini's Ethiopia they can quickly disillusion
their minds.

We will agree to differ.

Eric E. Leigh further accuses me of missing the
point in his letter. Be that as it may, my offer
made to accompany him (minus a respirator) into
a mustard gas chamber still holds good.

**G. A. S.**
*Whitstable Times and Tankerton Press*
May 1, 1937

**RIDICULOUS POLITICS**

## FASCISTI PILLS

SIR — That Communism today is on our doorstep is an indisputable fact. I am sometimes asked, why does not the government suppress by drastic legislation the Communist schools? The Special Constabulary is a recognised government auxiliary body vested with constitutional authority if called out to assist the police. Why is not a similar recognition extended to the British Fascisti who combat Communism by every means?

**C. PULLEY, COLONEL**
**Associate member of the British Fascisti**
*Kent & Sussex Courier*
February 27, 1924

## SILLY BUGGERS

SIR — I consider that the Special Constabulary, to which I have belonged since soon after demobilisation, meets all the requirements of emergencies without any of the disabilities of such ridiculous bodies as the British Fascisti.

**GEORGE H. WALES**
*Kent & Sussex Courier*
September 19, 1924

## CONUNDRUM

SIR — The only ridiculous feature I can discern about the 'Fascisti' is its name, which sounds non-British to my ears and is to many a conundrum.

**C. PULLEY, COLONEL**
**Associate member of the British Fascisti**
*Kent & Sussex Courier*
September 26, 1924

## HAVING MACARONI, AND EATING IT

SIR — It appears from your report of the meeting at the Drill Hall last week that Under-Secretary of State for Air Sir Philip Sassoon desires the Fascists in Folkestone to adopted a British name for their movement, but General R.J. Blakeney defends the Italian one on the ground that people eat macaroni.

As a peace-loving Labourist apprehensive lest such a divergence of opinion between the leaders of so militant a movement should lead to bloodshed, I should like to suggest that the name of Farcists would meet the difficulty— retaining the Italian, or macaroni, appearance and flavour, while being sufficiently British as to convey a general idea of the character of the movement.

Annandale defines 'farce' as 'a dramatic composition of broadly comic character; a comedy full of extraordinary drollery;

ridiculous parade; empty pageantry; mere show.'

I offer the suggestion for what it may be worth. It is possible, of course, that the Fascists may not have the necessary sense of humour to appreciate what a suitable name Farcists would be. Indeed I very much question if it would be so applicable if they had.

**C. RANDOLPH-LICHFIELD**
**Chairman of the Hythe Labour Party**
*Folkestone, Hythe, Sandgate, and Cheriton Herald*
December 20, 1924

## FROM A FASCIST 'FRIEND'

SIR — I have recently had some pamphlets of the Fascist movement sent me by some friends of mine in the British Legion, who have joined up with the former. The Fascist movement was organised to combat another movement—Communism—whose one aim and object is class war and eventual overthrow of the British Empire as we know it to-day. Its pamphlet, No. 1, reads as follows:—'It is not a class movement. It embraces all grades of society. Nor is it concerned with any shade of party politics, its ranks being open to all who are willing conscientiously to uphold its principles, i.e. the safe-guarding of the British Constitution from alien aggression and rule.' For the military heads of the movement—the gallant gentlemen who, without personal consideration, faced the worst in the Great War, that the women and children of this country might be saved from the horrors which befell the civilian population of France and Belgium—the safety of their country comes first. An extremist rising of Communists in this country is not so impossible. The French town of Amiens narrowly averted it this last week.

**EX-PRIVATE**
*Folkestone, Hythe, Sandgate, and Cheriton Herald*
December 27, 1924

## SHIRTY

SIR — I was quite unimpressed by the Blackshirtism at Mayfield. Consciously Hitlerish the speaker said 'Always it is we who are attacked. Always it is the Communists who attack us', then he expressed the fervent wish their leaders would give permission to retaliate. God save us.
**ALOE**
*Kent & Sussex Courier*
June 15, 1934

## FLUTTERY

SIR — I insist that I have never had any personal animosity towards Jews. Mental alacrity is perhaps the Jews' first quality, and it is a tragedy that it does not seem to be coupled with the finest patriotic motives.

**G. E. DEBURGH WILMOT**
**British Union of Fascists**
*Kent & Sussex Courier*
November 9, 1934


## NATURAL-BORN FISTS

SIR — I was interested to read the comments of Mr H.J. Baxter in your last issue, regarding the Fascist rally at Olympia last June. He overlooks the fact that even Fascists are to be excused if in exasperation they vocally counter demonstrate against the shrieking harridans and howling alien sub-men, imported in their thousands to prevent decent British men and women from hearing a policy vital to the interests of their own country. The events of the evening, as Mr Baxter so rightly states, are now well known, thanks to the statements made in favour of the Blackshirts by well-known public men as the Right Hon. David Lloyd George, MP. Has he read the statements of the above? I doubt it. Included in this long list of reliable persons' evidence must be added that of doctors who attended the victims of Red violence. Their injuries were caused, in the main, by kicks in the stomach and groin, and slashes from razors. No evidence has ever been produced by any member of the audience of any injury received other than those caused to their faces by coming in contact with good British fists.

To the evidence given above, I need add but little, but perhaps I may say that I saw one Blackshirt girl slashed in the face with a razor. Her assailant, who looked like a Pole, received the chastisement he deserved. I also saw a Blackshirt who was suffering from severe abdominal injuries being rushed to the West London Hospital.

**PETER WHITTAM**
*Dover Express and East Kent News*
November 23, 1934

## HORROR FACE

SIR — We are very pleased that Mr Osmond Page, secretary of the Benenden Conservative Association, should have been recruited out of sheer disgust with old-gang ineptitude, cowardice and utter refusal to face up to our situation.

**A. K. CHESTERTON**
**British Union of Fascists**
*Kent & Sussex Courier*
February 8, 1935

## HONESTLY

SIR — The policy of the British Union towards religion is one of complete toleration. We believe that a man should have the right to practise his religion. Under a Fascist government in Britain there would be no interference in the affairs of the church.

**MARGARET COLLINS**
**British Union of Fascists and National**
**Socialists**
*Kent & Sussex Courier*
November 20, 1936

### PERSECUTION PIFFLE

SIR — Our policy with regard to the Jews is not one of persecution, neither is our policy based on race like the German one, nor does it ignore the Jews as in Italy. Our policy demands an attack on the great Jewish interests which dominate the financial world. If there existed in Germany a large black population with a former considerable influence the position would doubtless be the same as that of the Jews.

**J. A. MACNAB**
**British Union of Fascists and National**
**Socialists**
*Kent & Sussex Courier*
January 8, 1937

### BANKING OVERSIGHT

SIR — The late General Ludendorf was

travelling with an Englishman after the war.
Resentful at Germany's defeat, the famous
general said. 'We lost the war because of the
Jews.' The Englishman replied: 'And the cyclists.'
'Why the cyclists', asked the general. 'Why the
Jews' said the Englishman. The dictators of
British finance are: the heads of Treasury, the
Bank of England, the Big Five banks represent-
ing 90 of banking activities. As far as I know
there is not a Jew among them.

**LANGTON LIBERAL**

*Kent & Sussex Courier*
January 8, 1937

# DARK NIGGLES

## NAKED-LIGHT SHOCK

SIR — My wife and I took a walk last evening during the black-out and we were shocked to observe a strong naked light shining from the first floor window of a house in the neighbourhood. It shone forth like a beam from a light advertising a dwelling if not a town lay below. It is conceivable that bombing would have been concentrated in circles around the spot and possibly hundreds of houses, whose owners have gone to so much trouble blacking out, would have been demolished, including those of the alert (?) A.R.P. [Air Raid Patrol] officials.

We tried to find a warden, special constable or other official on patrol and even visited the nearest sandbagged police box. After 20 minutes of futile search I eventually rang the bell of the house, and before answering the door the light was partly screened, and after my request completely so.

If we are asked at some future time to pay for all our local A.R.P. activity, surely we are entitled to ask, why?

**OBSERVANT**

*Kent & Sussex Courier*
October 13, 1939

## VACANT EVACUEES

SIR — As one of the many civic evacuees to

your delightful town, we can quite understand why it is people complain that there is nothing on in Tunbridge Wells. Apart from the pictures what is there for anyone to do in the evening. Surely you have some sort of Entertainments Committee?

**INTERESTED**
*Kent & Sussex Courier*
November 10, 1939


## SINISTER BUMBLE FETTERS

SIR — Would it not be interesting to find out just why the public have got to put up with one of the most disgusting bus services in the country. For goodness sake let our Town Council put forward an official demand that at least 50 per cent of those buses taken off be re-instated. One can almost read Bumbledom into this sinister fettering of those who have to carry on under endless difficulties without these being increased by a warped mind.

**SUFFERER**
*Kent & Sussex Courier*
November 24, 1939


## WING FURY

SIR — A few days ago I bough at a Tunbridge Wells shop a nice-looking chicken. However, the

white meat proved to be quite tasteless and the dark meat was so unpleasant in appearance that it was simply thrown away. I was puzzled until, in dissecting a wing, I found a metal ring with the words 'Hungarian Produce' stamped on it obviously carefully concealed inside the wing.
**CONSUMER**
*Kent & Sussex Courier*
January 12, 1940

\*\*\*

### ANATOLIAN ICE FOLLIES
SIR — As a repetition of last week's road purgatory may be on us at any moment can no one tell the Borough Engineer that the way to clear snow off his main roads is to run snow ploughs continuously while snow is falling. To allow snowfall to remain for days until it is an icy mass is the height of folly. I can only compare the state of the roads to those village tracks that existed in the hinterland of Anatolia during the winters of the last war, though I am not sure that this is fair to our gallant ally, Turkey. One trembles to think what would have been the fate of those responsible under a totalitarian regime.
**H. H. M. SPINK**
*Kent & Sussex Courier*
February 9, 1940

## WORK, ANYONE?

SIR — There are many conclusions as to why the roads have been left in such an appalling condition, but perhaps the most charitable is to assume that there are no longer any unemployed in Tunbridge Wells and that therefore there was no one available to clear the snow away.

**N. CHALMERS**
*Kent & Sussex Courier*
February 9, 1940

## PASSCHENDAELE

SIR — Main streets recently presented a surface that would have gladdened the heart of any able-bodied tank, but ordinary drivers bumped into semi-consciousness.

**E. F.**
*Kent & Sussex Courier*
February 9, 1940

## SNOW SENSE

SIR — Have the Powers that Be forgotten Christmas 1938? Perhaps they were consoling themselves with the idea that lightening never strikes in the same place. I have found myself thinking with gratitude of the old crossing sweeper. He at least did enable one to cross the road without storming the barricades. I should like to suggest they adopt the Scout motto: 'be prepared'.

**MRS MAUDE ELIZABETH CALLARD**
*Kent & Sussex Courier*
February 9, 1940


## FREEDOM EXPRESS

SIR — I desire to respond to your correspondents being now a free man and no longer a public official whose mouth is sealed. The volume of snowfall over 57 miles of dedicated highways heaped up would approximate 800 average two-story houses in a row. This writer has not been to Anatolia, but assumes that there snowfall is a hardy annual whereas here it is only an occasional inconvenience. This writer unhesitatingly states that there are not sufficiently unemployed in the borough to deal by manual labour with such a fall in an appreciably short period. This writer, too, would quote the Scouts' motto 'be prepared'; to which might be added 'to pay'—or would the correspondent be one of many who would resent the addition of a few pence to the rates? May I quote remarks addressed to the aristocratic London parish of St James's: The Lord sent it and if you await His good time He will take it away.

**W. A. FARNHAM**
*Kent & Sussex Courier*
February 9, 1940

## SNOW QUEEN

SIR — I suppose I should be overwhelmed by the facts and figures in Mr Farnham's letter but I am not at all impressed. If there was such an addition to our rates we should probably bear it. It is hoped those concerned will appreciate their new champion who has taken up the cudgels.

**MRS MAUDE ELIZABETH CALLARD**
*Kent & Sussex Courier*
February 23, 1940

\*\*\*

## CARDING OUTRAGE

SIR — While returning from Southborough one night about 11:30 pm with my wife we were walking on the opposite side of the road to the Drill Hall and I was surprised we were not challenged and asked for our identity cards; had we been the same side as the sentry he would have stopped us.

**C. GAINES**
*Kent & Sussex Courier*
June 21, 1940

## BRACKEN INVASION

SIR — We are being urged to prepare now for

possible attempts at invasion for which Parachute
Troops might be employed. May I suggest that
the bracken in Eridge Park, Rusthall Common
and other open spaces should be cut at once, for
it affords excellent cover.

**F. ALFORD SNELL**
*Kent & Sussex Courier*
July 5, 1940


## UNIMAGINABLE BLOCKHEADS

SIR — I was in a packed building in Tunbridge
Wells and went to the emergency exit and found
it blocked up. One cannot understand people
being so stupid!

**J. P. B.**
*Kent & Sussex Courier*
August 30, 1940


## DOG JAM

SIR — In all parts of the town innumerable dogs
chase each other madly across busy roads or
meander causing buses and other traffic to
swerve. Owners who turn their dogs out of
doors to roam around all day should be
penalised.

**J. HOLMWOOD**
*Kent & Sussex Courier*
September 7, 1940

## TWILIGHT FURY

SIR — If economy in fuel is vital to the nation's
war effort why is electric light being wasted in
our streets every night and all night long, moon
or no moon, raid or no raid.

We are all trying to do without that 60 watt bulb,
but surely the local Council should set an
example. How many tonnes of fuel are used on
this twilight lighting each night and why all night?

**PUZZLED**

*Kent & Sussex Courier*
August 14, 1942

## UMBRELLA DAMAGE

SIR — Can I mention a matter which I think
needs attention in our town, especially the
Tankerton end. A number of people have trees
in their front gardens which overhang the
pavement and are often so low as to come into
contact with heads, hats and umbrellas. In the
present 'black-out' conditions this is particularly
troublesome. I feel sure that this can and will be
rectified if the trouble is realised, but it must be
done by the householder I suppose, though I
have reason to believe that the local Council
ought to help.

**A DAMAGED 'BLACK-OUT' WALKER**

*Whitstable Times and Tankerton Press*
November 11, 1939

## LILY-LIVERED FUMERS

SIR — From time to time it is unfortunately necessary to draw public attention to the conduct of members of the community who treat by-laws of railway companies with disdain and consider themselves justified in using compartments which are labelled 'No Smoking' for the gratification of the smoking habit in complete disregard of the rights or comforts of other travellers.

Sometimes these people ask occupants of 'non-smoking' compartments if they object; more often they proceed to light up without any reference to their neighbours, and appear to be very surprised and hurt if anyone ventures to put them right.

The nuisance (for it certainly is a nuisance to be compelled to inhale the product of a smoker's indulgence in the confined space of a railway compartment) has been on the increase since the inauguration of the black-out. By their connivance the Companies are defrauding their non-smoking customers.

May I suggest that it is the duty of all non-smokers to protect against any infringement of the by-laws? It seems useless to expect offenders to play the games on their own initiative.

**SEASON TICKET HOLDER**
*Kent & Sussex Courier*
January 5, 1940

## 93 YARDS OF BLARING

SIR — It is natural at this time of year to have windows thrown open, but radio enthusiasts should remember that they cause an intolerable nuisance with blaring sets. Many in fact are a curse to their neighbours. It is always something of a mystery how the set owners can themselves put up with a programme turned on at full volume, but when one home is bracketed by two sets blaring alternative programmes the effect on victims is maddening. I took the trouble the other day to measure the distance one programme could be heard. I could still hear every word of the 9 o'clock news at the corner of the road 93 yards away. It is completely unnecessary and in most cases due to thought-lessness. While I appeal to householders to tone down the volume of their sets, I would remind them that action can be taken against the owners of noisy sets.

**FED-UP**

*Whitstable Times and Tankerton Press*
July 12, 1941

## BIN WARS

SIR — What is the exact Law concerning placing obstructions on the footpaths? In this town, refuse bins have to be put out on the pavement for refuse collection. This is the only town, to my knowledge, in which such a by-law is in force. The question is 'What authority is there behind this by-law?'

In our road the Council have for a second time been forced to postpone a necessary improvement begun before the last war, by the World War, just when full plans were being executed. There is practically no footpath at all in the west end of this road, on either side, and, in parts, none whatever. In the latter case the by-law cannot be observed—which is absurd. I have been told to place my bin on my steps, and am awaiting an order to put it in my bedroom.

On my steps, I am liable for possible accidents; on the pavement the Council is liable, not probably, but almost certainly. The accommodation roads are planned on this estate for all public services, amenities and utilities—e.g. gas, electric lights, drains (these are there) and sanitary collections. Accidents could not occur there to anyone's responsibility except of the injured. Houses were purchase on this understanding, and failure to comply is with the Council.

One might have added a further 'attraction' to a sea-side resort, of miles of poles and wires, the latter of which should have been underground from their inception.

**RATEPAYER**
*Whitstable Times and Tankerton Press*
March 27, 1943

## SPA KILLERS

SIR — While warmly approving the excellent schemes for making Tunbridge Wells a spa, I must confess that I see no likelihood of attracting any desirable newcomers to within ten miles of the Pantiles so long as the town permits such hideous noise on the Common to continue for weeks on end. Even if the presence of the Fair is inevitable, it is quite unnecessary that the enormous volume of the amplifiers employed should be allowed to spoil the amenities of an excellent town.

This distorted din can be heard as far away as Calverley Park and Forest-road—at times even in Rusthhall and Langton—and constitutes a public nuisance which the Town Council should surely exercise some control.

**ROY DOUGLAS**
*Kent & Sussex Courier*
June 9, 1940

## WEED HELL HOLES

SIR — The Statutory Allotments Committee of the Whitstable Urban District Council have recently received many complaints from house-holders and tenants of allotments of the nuisance caused by the scattering of the seeds of weeds growing without restriction in neighbouring gardens and allotments.

In response to the urgent request by the Ministry of Agriculture and Fisheries, thousands of householders have devoted their energies to the cultivation of vegetables, in many cases sacrificing their flower gardens and lawns, in the national effort to produce more food.

In addition to this a large number of vacant plots of lands have been taken over by Local Authorities for war-time allotments, and these are being cultivated by men, women and school children in the very little time at their disposal, as so many are engaged whole-time on war work or work part-time on the various branches of civil defence.

It is very disappointing to these people to see their crops spoilt by the scattering of seeds from their neighbours weeds and grasses, which disfigure their well-prepared vegetable beds.

**A. BERTRAM,**
*Whitstable Times and Tankerton Press*
July 11, 1942

## TUT TUT

Enclosed is a copy of a letter written to Whitstable Urban District Council which I hope will, in some measure, help to open their eyes to their responsibilities:

As, no doubt, you are aware, the

Government is urging all who can to avoid travelling this summer, especially holidaymakers. It will be seen that a great number of towns have already commenced their campaign of 'Holiday at Home,' and have an ideal programme drawn up which will keep in full swing until the end of September, and in these cases there would appear to be nothing lacking to attract the townsfolk beyond the measures of their own areas.

I know we cannot do quite all that other larger towns are doing, but I feel that a great deal could be done. The Whitstable Castle gardens which looked such a picture in peacetime have now deteriorated greatly. It has been suggested that band concerts be given on Sunday afternoons and evenings in the dancing enclosure. You will recall this was extremely popular just before the outbreak of war, and I might point out that the floor is still practically new and had been unused since dancing ceased in September, 1939.

More could be done in the way of advertising and attracting people to the tennis courts and bowling green, whose patrons, I fear, have dropped to a minimum. There could be weekly Talent Nights for the men and women of H.M. Forces. There must be untold talent of every kind suitable for entertaining their fellow troops and the civilians in the town, and it would give the soldiers something more to look forward to in their free evenings.

**WINIFRED J. SELLS
HAZEL TUTT**
*Whitstable Times and Tankerton Press*
June 20, 1942

\*\*\*

## EMPIRE SAVIOUR

SIR — At a time when the very existence of the Empire is at stake through the breaking of God's laws, and especially the fourth Commandment [Remember the Sabbath], it is hardly the time to add to the nation's sins. Surely men who are likely to face death at any moment need something better to meet eternity with than amusement. And, even if they must be amused up to the late hour of life, six days to do so ought to be sufficient, without encroaching on the Lord's Day.
**M. E. WELLDON**
*Kent & Sussex Courier*
February 23, 1940

## WAR BORES

SIR — We serving soldiers have followed the controversy over Sunday cinema in Tunbridge

Wells with amusement. Many of us feel that by
entering a cinema on a Sunday evening we should
be committing nothing wrong particularly during
this so far 'monotonous' war. Furthermore, we
call ourselves Christians and can and do go to
church on Sunday mornings when leave permits.
**SOLDIER BOY**
*Kent & Sussex Courier*
February 23, 1940

\*\*\*

## MALE COURAGE

SIR — Many of your readers will have heard the
story of Mrs Smith from the BBC recently, and
swelled with British pride at her carrying on after
three successive 'bombings out.' We Wardens
come across many such Britons in our frequent
calls at homes. Let me relate the story of a Mr
Jones who lives in my sector. Months ago I
invited him, an able-bodied, retired man, to
become a Warden, only to get the 101 excuses
which are so familiar to us. So I called myself, as
this unit had only one other available fit man.
This time a point blank refusal. The fire unit
captain appealed to him, all to no purpose.
**SENIOR WARDEN**
*Whitstable Times and Tankerton Press*
February 22, 1941

## BARBED FEATHERS

SIR — In the early days of the last war, my second son, Jack, joined the Royal Flying Corps. After several years' service, he was invalided out and a silver badge given him for his war service. One day, when walking down the street, a middle-aged lady gave him a white feather. The boy was astounded, and for some time failed to realise what it meant. Then tears welled up in his eyes and streamed down his cheeks. He opened his coat and showed his badge. The woman snatched the feather out of his hand and said: 'My poor boy; I am so sorry.' A short time after that poor Jack died in a military hospital in Ipswich.

**FRANK LAURENS**
*Kent & Sussex Courier*
January 16, 1942

## ROOF SCRAPERS

SIR —A short time ago the Secretary of State for Air announced that low flying over populous areas was forbidden. A surprise visit to Tankerton would convince him to the contrary. We are regularly subjected to 'roof scraping,' and even lower flights; while machine gunning of a target takes place regularly over the beach and, occasionally, over the town. With the Thames Estuary on one side and miles of open country on the other, there seems little reason why.

It is good to have peace between the nations. We would like now to be able to enjoy peace at Tankerton.

**ALBERT A. NORTH**

*Whitstable Times and Tankerton Press*
October 20, 1945

# A TOUCH OF CHARITY

## YARD STICK

SIR — In the opening of the late meeting held at the Town Hall on the Wednesday-Afternoon [Shop] Closing Movement, a letter was read from Mr J. Hollingworth, who was 'confident it would add many smart Young Men to the Rifle Corps.' Can any of your numerous readers inform the public how many recruits were added, and whether the yard measure was to be the formidable weapon?

**LOOKER ON**

*Maidstone Telegraph Rochester and Chatham Gazette* July 27, 1861

## MUSICAL MEDICINE

SIR —Within the last few years the taste for music has been greatly increased in England, in consequence of the formation of Sunday bands, such as we have in the parks of the metropolis and in some of the provincial towns. I think a great benefit would arise from the formation of a band in the town of Maidstone. Its civilising influence cannot for a moment be questioned, nor its moral effect upon the social condition of the workman, who, instead of wasting his money, his time, and his constitution in a public house, would be increasing his store of knowledge by listening to the strains of Mozart, or Beethoven,

or any other foreign or English master.
He would also invigorate his health and improve
his constitution by imbibing the pure atmosphere
instead of sour beer and other impurities. His
wife and little ones, too, might be made participa-
tors in the enjoyments, whereas, now, they are
sufferers. The money saved from the public
house would procure them apparel fit to appear
in public. An example would be set his children
that in matured years they would necessarily
profit from. I trust that this suggestion may lead
to some one carrying it into effect, and that if
you cannot prevail on men to attend chapel or
church, persuade them to come into green field,
that they may 'look through nature up to nature's
God'—anywhere but the public house.
**TEMPERANCE**
*Maidstone Telegraph, Rochester and Chatham Gazette*
February 9, 1861


## TEETOTAL FOUNTAINS

SIR — I cannot think that the Corporation did
quite right in appointing the fashionable hour of
3 pm for inaugurating the handsome fountain
now devoted to public use in the High-street.
Public fountains are springing into existence on
all hands. Great praise is due to the benevolent
persons at whose expense they are erected; but if
the class of individuals for whose especial benefit
so great a blessing is thus freely offered had been

consulted, the working men of the town would
have replied, 'We cannot afford to lose half a
day's labour; why not make the hour 12 o'clock
and let us all rejoice together.'
It is stated by the authorities that a public
execution is a lesson by which the people ought
to profit. That lesson is taught at noon, and if
our worthy corporation had set the example of a
'glass of water' at the same hour I think the
pattern would not have been without its effect.
**WALKER**
*Maidstone Telegraph*
November 1, 1862

## CANTERBURY MALES

SIR —The authorities of Canterbury leave
undone those things which they ought to do and
do those things which they ought not to have
done. The Stour is the main drain of an extensive
valley, and upon the proper cleansing, deepening,
and embanking of it depend the sanitary
conditions of the valley and its large population.
As the river runs it is the receptacle for every
kind of hard rubbish. There is a large soap
manufactory which now discharges the whole of
its spent lime and soap lees into the river, causing
the whole stream to have the colour and
consistency of lime wash twice or thrice a week.
Other filth is daily discharged into the stream.
Should we have heavy rains of fall of snow with

rapid thaws, the valley in the city will certainly be overflowed, flooding the houses of the poor in the lower parts of the city.
**CIVIS**
*Kentish Gazette*
July 28, 1863


## ROLL RAGE

SIR — I believe there is no place in the world where liberty is more justly claimed and maintained than in the ancient town of Dover. Still, there are a few interlopers who busy themselves to vent their ill nature.

I have, for a considerable time, been acquainted with a very respectable man who several years since suffered from paralysis following an accident which entirely disabled him, who is thus unable to move about except by means of a chair on wheels. His daily resort was the corner of Alexandra Place, London Road, where his patient manner and cheerfulness were warmly appreciated by numerous friendly passers by. To his great astonishment, however, he was served with a notice to cease visiting the spot as 'an obstructor of the thoroughfare.'
**OBSERVER**
*Dover Express and East Kent News*
May 19, 1911

## CYCLE GUARDS

SIR — At a time, like the present, when so many are asking 'what can I do for the men?' may I be allowed to enumerate a few articles which they would appreciate. Cardigan jackets, sweaters, mufflers, gloves, mittens (all Khaki for preference), flannel shirts and body belts, woollen vests, housewives and handkerchiefs, among other things, are absolute necessities and would be especially welcome. 'E' (Tunbridge Wells) Company of the Kent Cyclist Battalion has a lengthy stretch of Kentish Coast to guard, bleak and exposed, and withal highly dangerous from a 'landing' point of view. The men are in a very fit and hard condition from many hours entrenching daily. But the nights are becoming decidedly cold, and, if the men are to withstand the exposure during the long night watches and wet weather, warm clothing is essential.

**E. S. WALMSLEY**
*Kent & Sussex Courier*
August 21, 1914


## BELGIAN BLANKETS

SIR — I shall be glad if you will kindly allow me to thank all, who so generously responded to my appeal for blankets and clothing for Belgian refugees, now working in the hops gardens.

**WILLIAM KILFORD**

*Dover Express and East Kent News*
September 18, 1914

## ENGRAVED

SIR — The appeal to sportsmen to lend their race, field or stalking glasses for the use of officers under orders for the front has been most gratifying. Up to the present 18,000 pairs have been received. These have been examined and classified by an expert before being issued. The names and addresses of the owners are registered and the glasses themselves are engraved with an index number that the owners can be traced at the conclusion of the War and where possible returned.

**AILEEN ROBERTS**

*Dover Express and East Kent News*
January 1, 1915

## CIGARETTE AID

SIR — Will you kindly acknowledge the 11,700 cigarettes sent to me for the benefit of the wounded arriving at the Admiralty Pier. We have sent down in all 58,395 cigarettes collected in the town.

**VIOLET HOWDEN**

*Dover Express and East Kent News*
August 27, 1915

## LADY COMFORT

SIR — In a letter from a German prison camp, Private Denison, 2 Sherwood Foresters, says:— 'We are in rags; do send us warm clothing of any kind, and boots or clogs.' May I appear for the 450 men of my son's regiment imprisoned, for any warm cast-off men's clothing? I will make up parcels and send them to the camp at once. Already I have a few friends who have helped me, and shall gratefully acknowledge any more parcels sent to me here.

**MRS M. M. SHERBROOKE**

P.S.—I should like also to mention that to belong to the 'Comforts' Club' for soldiers, ladies send one article a month.

*Folkestone, Hythe, Sandgate, and Cheriton Herald*
October 16, 1915

## SEX TALKS

SIR — The most impressive report in a recent issue of the horrible fate of the late Sarah Walker is sufficient to make one ask: are we doing our part to prevent the possibility of so awful a condition in a human being? Could it not be, if not wholly, yet in part, prevented by courses of lectures being given at the Young Women's Christian Association and among men at meetings of the various brotherhoods and other societies?

Sex problems ought not to be tabooed from any false idea of modesty. Hundreds of thousands go wrong from want of knowledge. The case of Sarah Walker, 'one more unfortunate' dead at 19 years of age! Surely the Coroner's and Medical Officer's remarks at the inquest will lead to more light being given, especially to the youth of both sexes.

The officer in command of this district has the power to place 'out of bounds' all parts of the district where evil results are likely to follow the visits of soldiers. He has the power to prevent females visiting the camps, unless they can produce special permits to the Garrison Police. If those steps were taken now the Medical Officer at Lyminge Workhouse Infirmary would have fewer cases of the diseases which he so strongly referred to; and I therefore appeal to the churches and to the Town Council to bring immediate pressure to bear and so protect both sexes from the horrible results of promiscuous sexual indulgence.

**JOSEPH RIDGWAY**
*Folkestone, Hythe, Sandgate, and Cheriton Herald*
December 11, 1915


### BUFF CRAWL

SIR — According to rumour there is a

probability of our county regiment returning home at an early date and is likely to be stationed at Dover. There is no need to dwell upon the great historic traditions of our famous Buffs— traditions that have been maintained from 1572 to 1919 with unflinching valour and devotion on practically every battlefield where British blood has been shed. We read of the great reception already given to the Guards in London, and to be given shortly to London regiments. With the Guards, The Buffs can also fix their bayonets and march through London with drums beatings and colours flying, and require no mayoral authority of them to do so, and can claim the distinction of being the oldest regiment in the British Army. What are we going to do?

Are we going to allow the finest regiment in existence to crawl into Dover unobserved after all they have suffered for England and their home, Kent? Something must be done to give them a reception worthy of their splendid record. Let us see their colours flying and drums beating through our own streets, and our Kentish lads cheered by an enthusiastic population. It must be a welcome that will live forever in the ears of those who receive it.

**J. E. ENWRIGHT**
*Dover Express and East Kent News*
April 11, 1919

## STOUT HELP

SIR — May I once again appeal through the medium of your journal for a further supply of stout walking sticks, magazines, books, papers, etc., for our wounded soldiers landed at Dover? These articles are most urgently required at the present time. The magazines, etc., are placed on hospital trains, and are a source of great comfort to our men who had to travel long distances. I shall be pleased to fetch any goods on receipt of a post card

**W. J. MOOR**
*Dover Express and East Kent News*
August 6, 1920

## OUR BOYS IN INDIA

SIR — I am writing this on behalf of two or three of the old Dover 'boys' in my battalion. We are in South India, and in a very lonely spot with hardly anything to do, and should be pleased if some of your readers could kindly send us some reading material, as all we have to do when finished our duties is to sit in our barrack room and read.

**F. PAGE**, Belgaum, South India
*Dover Express and East Kent News,*
August 6, 1920

## WAR FALL-OUT

SIR — May I ask for space to rectify a somewhat misleading statement in the recently published fifth annual report of the Ministry of Pensions. This is that the metal artificial leg can only be supplied in the case of high amputations. On taking this matter up with the Ministry of Pensions, I am informed as follows: 'the Desoutter pattern duralimin leg and other light-metal legs have been adopted not only for high amputations, as stated in the fifth annual report of the Ministry of Pensions, but also for all about knee amputations where a pensioner is handicapped in his activity or occupation, and for all below knee amputations where the surgical aspect of the case renders a wooden limb unsuitable.'

Also I should like to add that provision has now been made for every applicant for a light metal limb to be referred to the limb fitting surgeon of his area. Should any wearers of artificial legs, or those interested in their supply, desire further particulars of the recommendations of the Williamson Committee, or on any other point arising out of the above information, I shall be happy to give it to them.

**HENRY H. C. BAIRD**

*Dover Express and East Kent News*
June 22, 1923

## YPRES DAY, 1924

SIR — The Committee of the Ypres League are deeply grateful to the cinemas of South-East Kent for their co-operation in the recent appeal organised in connection with Ypres Day, October 31. The appeal consisted of the sale of our song, 'A Corner of Flanders,' and the response, both from the public in purchasing copies, and from the cinemas in lending their aid, has been most gratifying.

**E. THOMPSON**

*Folkestone, Hythe, Sandgate, and Cheriton Herald*
November 8, 1924

## CHARITY CHEER

SIR — May a new resident in the town express his enthusiasm upon the balance sheet of the Brotherhood of Cheerful Sparrows hospital fund.

**PERCY ELLISON**

*Folkestone, Hythe, Sandgate, and Cheriton Herald*
November 8, 1924

## BOVRIL HELP

SIR — I am starting a fund to provide Bovril for our soldiers who are suffering so greatly from exposure in the trenches. By arrangement with the War Office, the Bovril will be dispatched without delay, and distributed equally. I am delighted to say that I already received support which has enabled me to supply over 10,000 cups of Bovril.

**GLADYS STOREY**
*Dover Express and East Kent News*
December 25, 1924

### BROTHER CARE

SIR — May I make an appeal on the behalf of Mr G.W. Hallett of Tunbridge Wells who, through a serious illness, is unable to follow his occupation and has 12 children to provide for; seven of these, through tender years, are unable to earn anything, the youngest being only two months old. Mr Hallett served through the South African War as a trooper in the 10th Royal Hussars, and was posted to the 2nd Buffs (East Kent Regt). Surely, sir, enough money has been collected at various times on behalf of ex-Servicemen that something can be done in this deserving case?

**CHARLES H. HALLETT**
*Kent & Sussex Courier*
October 16, 1925

### TOY RAGE

SIR — In reply to the letter of the Secretary of the Dover Unemployed Organisation in your last issue, I still maintain that to expend two thirds of the money collected on toys is out of all proportion.

**G. M. NORMAN**
*Dover Express and East Kent News*
March 23, 1934

### EGG RACE

SIR — Eggs are cheap at this time of the year, and for this reason they are being collected during the month of April by the Scouts, and many other helpers, from those who wish to give to the Hospital. The eggs are preserved, and are found most useful during the following twelve months when the price is higher. Thus every egg given now is really worth more than it costs at the present moment. This scheme has been in operation for many years in neighbouring towns with results varying from 11,000 to 32,000.'

**F. H. MORECROFT**
*Dover Express and East Kent News*
March 30, 1934

### STREET SWEEP

SIR — Those who have been present at the Pump Room can hardly doubt that what has been attempted was well worth doing. Each Sunday evening some 300 to 400 young people

have been attending who would otherwise have
been wandering about. They have been provided
with a variety of entertainment, including
concerts, films, lantern pictures and on one
occasion a nativity play.

**T. G. GILLING-LAX**
*Kent & Sussex Courier*
April 13, 1934

QUIRKS

## MINUTE MAD

SIR — In the account of the performance of the Diamond steam vessel, which I sent you last week, I simply sent a statement of facts as they occurred, and which were witnessed by upwards of a hundred persons who were on board the Comet; and let any one come forward and deny, if they can, what I there stated. There were also many highly respectable persons on Gravesend Pier who witnessed the arrival of the Diamond *ten minutes* ahead of the Comet and *not* 'four and a half minutes,' as stated in your editorial remarks. Now, Sir, there is an old adage that 'seeing is believing;' but while there are so many persons that would rather shut their eyes than see the truth, it is necessary to appear such a different mode of satisfying their doubts. Wagers are said to be foolish arguments—be it so—I propose to back the Diamond for 100l to 50l against the Comet, or any other steam vessel afloat (except the Star which has almost double the power of the Diamond) and which vessel has not been tried since the addition of her improved bow, in a run from Blackwall to Nore and back.

**AQUATICUS**
*West Kent Guardian*
February 21, 1835

## POMPOUS ASS

SIR — Your previous edition reads: 'One day last week, a low radical, ill-looking fellow, a friend of the magistrates, came reeling from the tap room of some pot house, mounted his horse (poor animal), and had the effrontery to ride on the Town Pier (which was at the time half filled with ladies and children), and fastened his horse to the rails for nearly an hour. The police took no notice of the circumstance; and yet several of the council were present.'

As there is no doubt that this paragraph is intended to apply to myself, and, as it is in all its defamatory particulars utterly false, I now call on you to inform me of the name of the author, in order that I may extract a due apology. If this demand is not accede to within three days, I shall forthwith commence an action against the proprietors of the *West Kent Guardian*.

[We refrain from giving the subscribed name to this letter, as we have no doubt the writer would be unwilling to have it publicly associated with the paragraph of which he complains. Knowing little of the gentleman, we are not prepared to offer an opinion whether his physiognomy or his politics tally. We should have had no disinclination in giving up the name of our informant, if it had not been required under a threat of action — to which

we profess ourselves wholly indifferent.—Ed.]
**ANONYMOUS**
*West Kent Guardian*
June 17, 1837


## VANISHING

SIR — The death of James Walters, aged 50 years, by the recent collision of the Topaz Gravesend steamer and the collier-brig Beacon of Sunderland, the coroner passed strong remarks upon the party who picked up the body disappearing.

I am the person who picked up the deceased. I wish to state I was not aware that there had been an inquest held until reading an account in your valuable paper, when I immediately walked up to Blackwall with my name and address written on three different pieces of paper, and handed them over to one of the Gravesend boats, requesting the captain to make it a public as possible.
**HENRY TEMPLE**
*West Kent Guardian*
September 4, 1841


## ROSETTA STONED

Professor W. Programme, a Fellow of the Obscure Society of Edinburgh, and of other societies, is engaged to present in the Painted Hall of Greenwich Hospital lectures on the *Simultaneous* System. This system is so new that nobody but himself knows anything about it. The intervals shall be accurately measured by a pocket sun-dial, the Professor's own invention, as serviceable by candlelight as day-light.

> *Practical seamanship*: The Professor's acquaintance with this science was gathered chiefly in the course of a long and tedious voyage from Scotland in a Leith smack. As an additional stimulus, he offers to perfect those interested on his contemplated return to his native country, by the same route.
> *Philology*: French, Latin, Greek, Hebrew, and Broad Scotch are rendered as easy as one's mother tongue. The Professor will trace such a word as quack to its original root, that it is strictly analogous to the quack of a goose; and that from hoax comes *hocus pocus*.
> *Political economy*: the Professor will show that the great principle of the Division of Labour is that everybody should do everything.

The final course will comprise a little bit of this thing—a little bit of that thing—and a little bit of t'other thing. The whole to wind up with a flourish, in the Professor's well-known style.

**PROFESSOR W. PROGRAMME**

*West Kent Guardian, Greenwich, Woolwich, and Deptford Courier, Rochester and Chatham Standard, & Gravesend and Milton Express*
January 22, 1842

## TURNIP KNIGHT SLUR

SIR —The Committee of the Greenwich Institution may be right or may be wrong—one of the two undoubtedly they are. 'Rise *Sir* Furnival Jenkinson Stalks' was uttered not in consequence of my labourers in Newfoundland, but solely on account of my exertions, after years of difficulty and perseverance, in rearing the turnip in the Island Mootoo woo. Possession is nine-tenths of the law, and why should the Committee trouble themselves about the other tenth—whether they do their duty or please members?

**FURNIVAL JENKINSON STALKS**

*West Kent Guardian*
November 11, 1848

## HARE EXTRAORDINAIRE

SIR — The readiness with which you insert

letters relating to the sports of the field has
induced me to present you with the following
extraordinary run on Wednesday last.

The meet was at Broomfield, in the Herne
country, where, shortly after half-past ten,
upwards of twenty horsemen assembled and,
after waiting a few minutes, we proceeded to look
over fields, and a hare was found, which was
killed, after a run of about an hour. We then
looked several fallows, until we got to a field
where a brace of hares got up simultaneously.
One of them we drove across the park into cover
on the other side, but could not make her go
away. Then the run of the season commenced.
Puss making away for the park, round which she
took a turn, and then to the tile kiln, and, skirting
the park again, here she waited, and the hounds
getting a view at her sent her straight away for a
little farm on the hill. The hare then went to the
right and here the pace began to tell on her, the
hounds raced her from scent to view, and she
made a double in the ditch, which gave her
another chance. Running the ditch about 100
yards she went to Chesterfield into a small ash
plantation, where the hounds were so close to
her that the master jumped off his horse and ran
into the plantation, thinking they had killed her,
but this proved a mistake for she escaped their
jaws, apparently as fresh as ever. We went straight
through into the West Blean. Here the hounds
ran into her and broke her up. I counted twelve
horses up to the finish, including the master's.

Time, one hour exactly.
**AN ISLANDER**
*Kentish Gazette*
February 1, 1859

## FEVER PITCH

SIR — I have been weekly expecting to see a
notice in the *Gazette* that the Cavalry Depot Band
has commenced playing on the Dane John for
the season. If such is the case, I hope you will
insert a short notice to that effect in your next
impression, stating also the day and hour of
performance, as doubtless many of your readers
would, like myself, occasionally come to hear it.
**J. D. NORWOOD**
*Kentish Gazette*
July 16, 1867

## PITY

SIR — Will you kindly allow me through your
columns to thank the public for the sympathy
shown to me for the loss of my child in the late
tram accident. Also to say that I am convinced it
was a pure accident which no driver could have
prevented.
**JOSEPH VOLLER**
*Dover Express and East Kent News*
July 7, 1899

## RADIO DUST

SIR — Having taken a stroll into Connaught Park last Friday, my attention was attracted by two enormous ribs forming an archway, which on closer examination proved to be from the jaw of the whale. Only a few years will suffice to transform these to their amorphous dust unless the ingenuity of man is exercised to protect them from the radio energies of the elements.

**UNEMPLOYED**
*Dover Express and East Kent News*
February 12, 1904

## BRAIN PAIN

SIR — On my return to Dover after a short absence, I found to my great surprise and regret that the historical custom of firing the salute gun at 12 mid-day and 9.30 pm, had been abandoned. This regrettable change is due to complaints made by inhabitants of East Cliff, that the concussion shook their pictures, windows and nerves. Having resided at East Cliff I can vouch for the absurdity of the statement.

**AN OLD RESIDENT**
*Dover Express and East Kent News*
May 13, 1913

## FAUX PAST

SIR — In reply to a letter in last week's *Herald*
written by one who thought that caricaturing
Napoleon in pictures was bad taste in a town like
Folkestone, where there are many French
visitors, may I say that this particular picture,
entitled 'Wiffles as Napoleon' was produced by
the foremost of French cinema companies,
namely, the Pathé Frères Cinema Company?
**PICTURES**
*Folkestone, Hythe, Sandgate, and Cheriton Herald*
October 4, 1913

## LITTLE GREEN MEN

SIR — If you meet a man or youth clad in green
or brown with a Saxon cowl upon his head, a
staff in his hand, and rucksack on his back, you
will know him a kinsman of the Kibbo Kift. All
those who are keen on the open-air life,
camping, and woodcraft should get in touch with
the 'man in green.'
**BROWN WOLF**
*Folkestone, Hythe, Sandgate, and Cheriton Herald*
February 23, 1924

## TOMB RAIDER

SIR — I have been very interested in the epitaphs on tombstones:

Ditchling Churchyard, Sussex:

> Here lyes honest old Harting,
> And snug close beside un,
> His fat wife, a wide one.
> If another you lack
> Look down and see Jack.
> And farther a yard,
> Lyes Charles, who drank hard.
> A near un is Moggy,
> Who never got groggy,
> Like Charles and her father.
> Too abstemious rather,
> And therefore popp'd off
> In a tissickey cough

St Nicholas Churchyard, Brighton:

In memory of Phoebe Hessell, born at Stepney in the year 1713. She served for many years as a private soldier in the 5 Regt. Of Foot in different parts of Europe. In the year 1745 fought under the command of the Duke Cumberland, at the Battle of Fontenoy. Her long life, which commenced in the time of Queen Anne, extended into the reign of George IV, by whose munificence she received support. She died

December 12, 1821. Aged, 108 years.

Very few quaint epitaphs seem to have been used during the past 30 or 40 years.
**T. C.**
*Folkestone, Hythe, Sandgate, and Cheriton Herald*
October 11, 1924

## FAMILY BOSOM

SIR — If your readers are not yet tired of curious epitaphs here are a few. Notice this one by a Frenchman who lost his wife:

> Tears cannot restore her,
> Therefore I weep.

Or this, by a wife on her departed husband:—

> May he rest in peace
> Until we meet again.

For terseness this one on a baby, who died a few hours after being born, would take some beating:

> Came in,
> Looked about,
> Didn't like it,
> Went out.

For brevity surely this could not possibly be

excelled:

He was.

**W. E. ROSE**
*Folkestone, Hythe, Sandgate, and Cheriton Herald*
September 6, 1924

## HANG ON

Grieve not for me, my husband dear,
I am not dead, but sleeping here;
With patience wait, prepare to die,
    And in a short time, you will come to I.

After a while, the following:

I am not grieved, my dearest life,
Sleep on—I've got another wife;
Therefore I cannot come to thee,
    For I must go and live with she.

**G. M. HAYWARD**
*Folkestone, Hythe, Sandgate, and Cheriton Herald*
October 11th, 1924

## CAPITAL 'FLU BUSTERS

SIR — I was brought up to think the capital a
rather unhealthy place, but one of the first things

I have noticed is the almost complete absence of an influenza epidemic although other parts of the country are affected. Whatever the reason, the popular custom here of taking a hot lemon drink at night and two or three oranges during the day seems very successful in warding off 'flu.

**MRS EDITH ROBERTSON**
*Kent & Sussex Courier*
January 13.1933

## DOVER DUELS

SIR — It is possible that there may be amongst the readers someone who can supply—from a diary, letter, or by other means—some details of the last duels fought in Dover. In 1836, the Society for the Suppression of Duelling was in existence, and in 1842 the last duel took place, Lieut. Seaton being killed.

**TACITUS**
*Dover Express and East Kent News*
June 2, 1933

## PAST TIMES

SIR — One day I was expecting a telegram from Liverpool informing me when a party was due to arrive by train at Euston Station, London. When I left home to catch the 9.40 am train from Maidstone East the telegram had not arrived.

There were four minutes to wait before the train was due to leave. Suddenly the station master looked in the compartment and said: 'Are you Mr——!' 'Yes.' He said: 'A phone message has just come from your house, sir, that the Liverpool train is due in Euston at noon.' I resumed my seat inexpressibly grateful.

**PROFESSIONAL MAN**
*Kent Messenger*
January 8, 1938


## DRINK-JERK BLUNDERS

SIR — I doubt the statement by Mr Ogden that total abstinence is necessary for the attainment of success in sport. One only has to recall the case of H. Cotton, former British Open Golf Champion. Previous to winning, Cotton was an abstainer and suffered from nervous dyspepsia induced by strain. His doctors advised him take a little light wine with his food: he is now our premier golfer. It is not necessary, either, to indulge in violent and prolonged jerks.

**W.H. STAFFORD**
*Kent & Sussex Courier*
September 1, 1939


## RAILWAY RUT

SIR — It was with great interest that I read your

recent article on the Canterbury-Whitstable railway. The difficulties over the tunnel, and the erection of the first railway bridge in the world, at present standing in Church Road, are historical items which have become too easily forgotten. The present decline in the railway-mindedness of the public should not be allowed to cloud the achievements of the nineteenth-century people— particularly now, as the twilight of the era they created is fast approaching.

**J. L. C TAYLOR**
*Whitstable Times and Herne Bay Herald*
July 1, 1950

## TWO GENERATIONS

SIR —I think my own case beats most records. It beats Lord North's by 20 years! Lord North is 91 and his grandfather was born 170 years ago; I am but 58 and my paternal grandfather was born 157 years ago! This is my record:—Grandfather (General Craufurd), born 1770 (killed 1815); father born 1804; myself born 1869 (youngest child).

**MRS L. M. BILL (NÉE CRAUFURD)**
*Dover Express and East Kent News*
September 9, 1927

SPORTS

## SHAME SPORT

SIR — A 'sportsman' took a purse containing £1 from my trousers pocket, whilst they were hanging in the Pavilion, on the Athletic Ground, on Saturday last. I should not mind about it so much myself, but when one has two depending on him for their living, it makes it come very hard.

**H. W. CULLEN**
*Dover Express and East Kent News*
May 23, 1913

## FUR AND FEATHER FUNK

SIR — What has become of the Folkestone Fur and Feather Show? This has in the past been a special feature of the town, and was recognised as one of the principal shows in the kingdom, but of late it seems to have dropped into oblivion. The last, held in 1911, was from enquiries made of the Secretary to the fanciers' society in Folkestone, not a financial success. Yet it seems that, in a growing town like this is, there should surely be enthusiasts enough.

**A FANCIER**
*Folkestone, Hythe, Sandgate, and Cheriton Herald*
December 6, 1913

## NOT CRICKET

SIR —I beg to inform you that the so-called St Barnabas Cricket Club is quite unauthorised and has no connection whatever with St Barnabas' Church.

**P. LUDGATE**
**St. Barnabas's Church Cricket Club**
*Dover Express and East Kent News*
June 13, 1919


## CRY-BABIES

SIR — I have witnessed several matches this season, both from the stand and from amongst the line spectators, and have formed the opinion that the position of the Club is as much due to the spectators as the players. The Folkestone ground is not alone where one hears the referee anathematised: 'what do we pay our bob for, referee?' If the Club wins, it wins on its merits, but if it loses, it is due to the unfairness of the referee.

Is that British sportsmanship? Professional football is not sport as I think most of us would like it to be. It is a commercial undertaking. However, it is here to stay, and we must all unite in making it a clean, manly British game. The Folkestone players must learn to take clean knocks and not cry. They could learn a lot from a schoolboys' match.

## A VISITOR AND A CLUB WELL-WISHER
*Folkestone, Hythe, Sandgate, and Cheriton Herald*
March 15, 1924

### GIRL FAUL

SIR — I see amongst the many comments made on Miss Ederle's Channel swim no mention made of the important fact, which, I understand is not denied, that she swam in the lee of her tug! This fact will, I think, account for a number of things which happened on this very remarkable swim, and, in my opinion, certainly puts any claim to swimming the Channel out of court. It is open to so many grave objections and possibilities of unfair practices, and the records must be like Caesar's wife 'above suspicion,' and no record should stand which is accomplished under these conditions. I raise this question because I have reason to believe that other swimmers are contemplating using the same method and it is time something was done.

**SPORTSMAN**
*Dover Express and East Kent News*
August 20, 1926

FLORA & FAUNA MYSTERIES

## DUMBFOUNDED

SIR — You know how fond I am of birds, in
fact, of all dumb animals. Some three weeks
back one of the wild pigeons in the Park had
been caught by some who tied its legs together,
making it quite lame. This morning, with the
assistance of Hopkins, we caught it and cut the
string away with great difficulty, it having cut
the leg, which was very much swollen.
Also about two months since someone had tied
some wire on to another bird very tightly on
part of the leg and foot. We could never catch
it, it being so frightened, I think, from the pain,
but a few days ago a portion of the foot came
away, and released the wire. It has now only one
claw, but I don't think it suffers any pain from
it. Who can be so cruel?

**J. ELDRIDGE**

*Folkestone, Hythe, Sandgate, and Cheriton Herald*
October 4, 1913

## PERFECTLY DEAD

SIR — I have been fortunate enough during
this week to have obtained in Kent some very
fine specimens of the caterpillar of the rare
death's head hawk moth. These measure from
4in. to 5in. in length, and are perfect
specimens.

**G. E. TOOK**
*Dover Express and East Kent News*
August 4, 1933

## CORN

SIR — The beautiful cornflower, the blue variety,
is a pretty flower and a flower which has many
associations. It is the German national emblem.
It has also the distinction of giving a name to a
colour, namely, cornflower blue. In Sussex it is
known as the cornthistle. Has Kent a name of its
own for the cornflower?

**REV. J. P. BACON PHILLIPS**
*Dover Express and East Kent News*
June 21, 1935

## LEPIDOPTERAN GLOOM

SIR — With reference to the Comma butterfly,
you may be interested to know that I took a
specimen in my garden here on Sunday. Knowing
Maidstone and district very well indeed, I venture
to say that Vanessa C. *album* has not been seen
there for a very long time. In fact, although I
have been interested in the British Lepidoptera
for many years, I have not previous seen it 'on
the wing.'

[The Comma has been introduced artificially in
Surrey, and that may account for the present state

of things.—Ed.]
**S. LANE**
*Dover Express and East Kent News*
August 10, 1934

## GENETIC LOUT

SIR — Surely Sevenoaks can claim an unusual proportion of albinos amongst its fauna. Apart from white blackbirds of which there have been several near hear in the past years, we have had a pure white rook that daily visited. Someone with a gun was said to be after it. At any rate, it disappeared after a few months.

A few years ago there was a white squirrel in Knole Park. Last autumn I saw one in Great Brittains Wood, but only once. The last few days a white squirrel has been frisking on some trees near my house. It permits close approach and I only hope it will not also fall a victim to the lout with a gun.

**JOHN DRUCE**
*Kent & Sussex Courier*
April 7, 1939

## KILLER INSTINCT

SIR — I venture to suggest that these rare White Admirals have, with the assistance of Britain's tempestuous summers, travelled further afield in search of fresh haunts. I am hoping to see that gem of gems, the Camberwell, and yet, in a way, I hope I do not, because I am morally certain that my collector's instinct would refuse to be suppressed.

**L. BANKS**

*Dover Express and East Kent News*
August 11, 1939

WITS END

## INSIDER KNOWLEDGE

SIR — To Mr Wade: excuse me if I do not follow your example of calling you uglier and blacker names than that you called me at your board meeting, last week. Then, because I write in a plain manner, my 'letter was written by some jail-bird, afraid to give up his name, lest a police officer would take him up.' You may be a good judge of the style of a 'jail-bird.' I am not.

**PAT ST NICHOLAS**

*West Kent Guardian*
August 23, 1851

## EMPTY SHELL

SIR —Zamoiski's Lectures excited the minds of hundreds of our townspeople; but I am sadly disappointed with the letter in your paper of Saturday last. Truth Seeker endeavoured to assist me out of a fog which he says I am in about the lectures. What an extraordinary capacious stomach he has, having swallowed mesmerism, electro-biology, clairvoyance, spiritualism, and table-rapping. Really? In plain English, your answer is devoid of any.

**R. BUCKNELL**

*Maidstone Telegraph, Rochester and Chatham Gazette*
March 9, 1861

## SHINGLE-MINDED

SIR — Your contemporary the *Observer* in its
account of the re-opening of the above Church
on Tuesday last says 'the roof of the tower is
cover with small *Deal shingle.*' Now, though the
traditional schoolboy need not be told, still there
may be some—your contemporary among the
rest—to whom the information will be useful,
that the material indicated is not to be found
with 'common objects on the sea shore.'

**X**

*Kentish Gazette*
December 21, 1869

## JACK MATE

SIR — We, the Labour Party in Hythe, are sorely
in need of a Union Jack to drape the front of the
speaker's table at our meetings, and in view of
the fact that our funds do not permit us to
indulge in luxuries, I am wondering whether
someone among our well-to-do opponents would
be willing to present us with one, and thus save
us from the unjust reproach that we do not
'stand by the flag.'

**C. RANDOLPH LICHFIELD**
**Chairman of the Hythe Labour Party**

*Folkestone, Hythe, Sandgate, and Cheriton Herald*
November 29, 1924

## WHO YOU?

SIR — I quite agree that schoolmasters should 'mind their own business,' and also that music teachers should follow the same rule. I assure Mr Lashmar that I am not 'sore about some his pupils being away from school for music lessons.' Until I saw his letter in your paper I had never even heard of him.

**RURAL EDUCATION**

*Kent & Sussex Courier*
July 17, 1925

## FROST BITE

SIR — With reference to 'Gardener' correspondent's letter in your issue of October 9, I have to point out that the fact of having ground frost does not prove the climate is 'Arctic.'

**PLUVIUS**

*Kent & Sussex Courier*
October 16, 1925

## MANNA MONEY

SIR — Our worthy Alderman Barwick referred to intoxicating beverages as 'the gifts which God had sent them.' Alcohol has its uses as a medicine, or a chemical, or a fuel for motors, but all good gifts of God are not given to be swallowed, or to be sold for the enrichment of great monopolies and their shareholders.

**C. W. MASON**

*Dover Express and East Kent News*
October 1, 1926